Creating Wealth

PRINCIPLES AND PRACTICES FOR DESIGN FIRMS

by Ellen Flynn-Heapes

·S·P·A·R·K·S·

THE CENTER FOR STRATEGIC PLANNING

For information contact:

SPARKS: The Center for Strategic Planning, P.O. Box 205,
Alexandria, Virginia 22313; Telephone: 703-838-8080;
Facsimile: 703-838-8082; E-mail: INFO@ForSparks.com;
Web: www.ForSparks.com.

First Edition

Book Design and Production: Wilton Daniels, Wilton House
Library of Congress Card Number: 99-91625

Printed in the United States of America
ISBN 0-9675696-0-5

CREATING WEALTH IS YOUR RIGHT.
GUARANTEED BY THE CONSTITUTION OF THE UNITED STATES.

A Toast

I'd like to thank the hundreds of firms that have generously shared their ideas, histories, and experiments. With your data points, we now have a better map to guide us into the future. I am hopeful that this book will pave the way for true leadership by our profession in the new millennium, as well as the personal rewards which are so richly deserved for such deep dedication.

A Note

Firms mentioned in this work are included by the author in good faith and based on published material, company sources, and personal observations. We recognize that firms change and grow every day, so characterizations may be imperfect. We beg your indulgence for this, and hope that you will allow a little leeway for our purposes, which are strictly educational.

CONTENTS

Focus is a concentrated effort to bring about outstanding
skill and contribution.
Not all clients are willing to pay for your kind of expertise.
The key is to match skill with client agenda.

CONTENTS

ACKNOWLEDGMENTS

Sincere thanks to those who took part in the creation of this book. First to our clients who are truly the source of inspiration. And always to those friends and colleagues who gave great advice and feedback, including Ray Messer, Ed Friedrichs, Jim Cramer, and Laurin McCracken.

Special thanks to Wil and Casey Daniels of Wilton House who provided excellent guidance and technical insight in the preparation of this book.

Finally to Richard and Elliott whose support was unwavering throughout the journey.

INTRODUCTION

Wealth is a great thing. It's the fuel that frees us to do anything we want: to meet any challenge with vigor, to build meaningful practices in areas that matter, to attract the best and brightest people, to be selective in our clients, and truly, to enjoy what life has to offer.

Wealth does not result from short-term tactics for beating the competition. Instead, wealth results from choice: the choice to be exceptional. *Creating Wealth* offers a simple yet breakthrough concept: *You must become MASTERFUL at something – a technology, a building type, a client type, a niche, a locale – something that you build to a high level of worth.* Only then are you in a position to truly create value, sustainable value, in the face of tough competition.

As management consultants to the design professions, we are in the trenches every day fighting against the depressing practices of mediocrity, underpricing, and over-serving. We work with firms across the country, and we see first hand the shortsighted, but well-intentioned, mistakes made by firm after firm. Most desperately try to run faster in the hamster wheel or grow as large as possible. But there are *many* other options.

I hope *Creating Wealth* will challenge your thinking and help you cultivate your own unique, valuable organization for the 21st century.

Ellen Flynn-Heapes, President
SPARKS: The Center for Strategic Planning

Chapter One

Wealth –
What a Concept!

PORTRAIT OF A MILLIONAIRE

The following portrait is from *The Millionaire Next Door*, by Thomas J. Stanley and William D. Danko. The authors are leading experts in the study of affluence, having dedicated themselves to the subject for more than 20 years. Note that this portrait reflects what they term "prodigious accumulators of wealth" rather than the more highly visible "big hat - no cattle" conspicuous consumers.

As you read these observations, ask yourself how you compare.

- We are self-employed. (Self-employed people make up less than 20 percent of the workers in America, but account for two-thirds of the millionaires.)
- Our household's annual realized (taxable) income is $131,000, our average income is $247,000, and our average household net worth is $3.7 million.

"People can be divided into three groups: those who make things happen, those who watch things happen, and those who wonder what happened."

John W. Newbern

- On average, our total annual realized income is less than 7 percent of our wealth. In other words, we live on less than 7 percent of our wealth.
- We live in homes currently valued at an average of $320,000. About half of us have occupied the same home for more than 20 years, and have enjoyed significant increases in its value.
- Most of us have felt at a disadvantage because we didn't receive any inheritance. About 80 percent of us are first-generation affluent.
- We live well below our means. We wear inexpensive suits and drive American-made cars. Only a minority of us drive current-model cars or ever lease a car.
- Our wives are a lot more conservative financially than we are.
- We have a "go to hell" fund. In other words, we have accumulated enough wealth to live without working for 10 or more years.
- Only about 17 percent of us ever attended a private school, although most of us are fairly well educated. Many of us hold advanced degrees.
- As a group, we believe that education is extremely important for ourselves, our children, and our grandchildren. We spend heavily on education for our offspring.
- Our kids should consider providing affluent people with some valuable service. We recommend accounting and law, tax advisory and estate planning.
- About two-thirds of us work between 45 and 55 hours per week.
- We are fastidious investors. On average, we invest nearly 20 percent of our household income realized each year.
- I am a tightwad. In fact, *I* am my favorite charity!

WHAT IS WEALTH AND WHY IS IT GOOD?

Most of the nation's wealthy own businesses, and their income derives primarily from their business. In the design industry, our practices are also our prime source of income. Whether businesses or practices, they serve the same purpose: to provide the vehicle to achieve our goals, whatever they may be.

Achieving goals and generating income are inextricably entwined. Yet somewhere along the line, often in our education, we miss this point. Kimley-Horn EVP Mike Byrd was teaching a class of recent college graduates when the subject of money and value came up. One student commented that if he wanted to make a lot of money, he would have become a doctor or a lawyer. "But money isn't the most important thing to me," the grad said, "Engineering is." Mike was proud of the new staffer's passion for the profession, but "it bothers me that someone believes he's going into a profession in which there is no opportunity to make money. As a profession, we may be our own worst enemy."

When we talk about "making money," what do we mean? What does business wealth look like? As the authors of *The Millionaire Next Door* point out, wealth is all about assets — assets that you faithfully build and convert into cash only as you need to.

What specifically constitutes wealth in the design industry? Some would answer quantitatively:

- A high book value: assets to liabilities
- A strong profit position such as consistently exceeding 33% net profit before distributions and taxes

- A high labor-to-revenue multiplier such as achieving a 4.0 net result
- A healthy growth rate such as averaging 25% per year

Some might answer qualitatively:

- A leadership position in the chosen expertise or market
- A well-recognized company name and stellar reputation
- A process for staying on top through innovation
- Many high performers who are fully engaged
- A client base who recognizes your value and is willing to pay for it
- An investment mentality directed toward strength-building systems, equipment, and people
- An ability to financially reward deserving staff
- A well-oiled work production process borne of knowing what you're doing

Some might offer quality of life factors:

- The ability to fund sabbaticals for principals or senior employees
- Reasonably balanced work and family life

Some might even offer "psychic profit," or the luxury we experience when we forego a financial reward in lieu of an emotional one such as the feeling of contribution derived from pro bono work. Psychic profit can also be found in the relief of pressure, such as not having to manage a sizable staff or freedom from intensive marketing.

Wealth can truly be defined in many ways. However, for our purposes, I will discuss wealth as Webster defines it: "all property that has a money value or an exchangeable value for *economic utility*..."

Is this view of wealth too crass and commercial for professionals? Some think not. Since ancient times, the exchange of money has been a recognition of value – for constructive and creative effort, for contribution to the economic well-being of others, and for marking the tangible evidence of a life's work. That *economic utility* confers two real benefits: freedom and control. With freedom and control, design professionals can reach a higher level of contribution to our 21st century society, and in turn, become more highly valued themselves.

WEALTH CRITERIA

Take a moment to compare your firm's assets to those in the list above. Give a grade using a scale of 1-5, and write a brief evaluation in the space that follows.

GRADE

"In the long run, men hit only what they aim at."

Henry David Thoreau

It Starts with an Aspiration

As Thoreau suggests, *aiming* is essential to hitting a target. Take a few minutes to think back on an aspiration you've had in your life, a goal you have aimed for. Maybe it was professional registration, marrying the spouse of your dreams, or attaining a certain net worth. Jot down a few notes in the margin about what you did and how you made it happen.

Reflecting on your experience, you probably learned something about boldness, focus, and discipline. You probably had to sweat some, risk some, let certain things go by the wayside, and make a few trade-offs. You probably had to apply some resources to your dream, whether time, money, or a combination. But when you achieved your goal, it was sweet, wasn't it? A moment you'll savor forever.

As a process, creating wealth uses the same basic principles and tools that you used to fulfill your dream.

Why Doesn't Every Firm Create Wealth?

Seven powerful paradigms reign in our industry. Some are useful, but others have a darker side that keeps us from launching ahead with vigor. See if any of the following fit the mindset of your firm:

Assumption #1:
Bigger Means We're Better (and Safer)
The last time you were introduced to a colleague in the industry, did you ask him how big his firm was?

The answer tells us the degree to which we should be impressed, or not. Every city has the list of the largest engineering firms, architectural firms, interior design firms. And we look to *Engineering News Record, Building Design & Construction,* and others for the national rankings by size of company billings.

True, most of us admire the large, name-brand firms. They seem powerful and weighty – real leaders among us. In reality, however, the profitability of many behemoths is consistently below industry average. "Large firms," says Bill Fanning, PSMJ's Director of Research, "perform about two percent below industry average, at the 30th or 40th percentile. Almost without exception, their profitability under-performs smaller firms." Why is this? Fanning considers the 16-cylinder Jaguar. "It may be cool, but it's tough to keep all those cylinders working in sync."

Why do we feel so strongly about being big? Corporate CEOs get significant rewards when they increase their company's size. The celebrated examples of Nations Bank and Bank of America, Mercedes and Chrysler, Citicorp and Travelers will always make front page news, but have they truly increased the value of their businesses? Plenty of unimpressive results are recorded later when they show poor performance due to inefficiencies, politics, and bureaucracy.

Although most of us seek size for good reasons, such as bench depth, an internal market for ownership transfer, project variety to keep staff challenged, and the ability to afford support staff, a slippery slope presents itself for those who get carried away with the frenzy. As marketing becomes a conveyor-belt process, they

"The merger of Travelers and Citicorp is the only place outside Jurassic Park you can watch dinosaurs mating."
Gary Hamel
Competing for the Future

speak bland messages to appeal to an ever-wider audience, forgetting the specific and personal. They accept more and more opportunities on the fringes of their value-creation expertise. Sometimes, they underprice and promise the moon to win the job, which leads directly to a downward commodity spiral.

Years later, they look back. Yes, they are large and well-known, but they wonder how they got trapped on such a high-risk/low-return treadmill.

"Growth for growth's sake is the ideology of the cancer cell."
Edward Abbey

Creating wealth requires the firm to be great at something, *not everything*. The end game is not volume, but distinction and contribution, which naturally lead to increased fees, increased respect, and increased control of schedule. Growing large may or may not follow as a result.

Assumption #2:
Diversification Will Help Hedge Our Bets
Most practitioners understand diversification to mean getting into *more* markets and services so as to hedge their bets if a market turns down. This is a misguided idea from a wealth-creating standpoint, especially if isn't done in a highly disciplined way.

Consider the many firms that acquire new offices in an effort at diversification. When cultures and skills are similar, they can be very effective. But too often, firms attempt to combine a new geography with a new expertise, such as the New York civil engineer who acquires a thriving landscape practice in Florida. Sometimes a well-focused firm will acquire a generalist practice in a target state, only to find that the fine local practice in Arizona can't sell the firm's national strength in preschools. Looks like sensible diversification that could yield synergies, but in fact, it proves very difficult to manage.

In a study conducted of 33 American corporations from 1950 to 1986, Michael Porter, recently voted the most influential living strategist, concluded that "diversification has done more to destroy shareholder value than to create it." Lee Iococca admitted that his biggest mistake with Chrysler was to diversify into Chrysler Motors, Chrysler Aerospace, Chrysler Financial, and Chrysler Technologies. GE, the world's largest conglomerate, dumped diversification (and half its workforce) in favor of being number one or two in each of its selected markets.

Perhaps the biggest surprise is that the focused spin-offs are doing much better than their parent companies.

Assumption #3:
Fortune 500 Advice Works for Us, Too
Much advice that we read about in the general business literature is intended for huge manufacturers and institutions with moribund, bureaucratic operations that employ minimum wage workers. Yes, we can learn from many sources, but corporate America can confuse us as easily as it can enlighten us.

Among the messages that we hear are: *Improve service. Practice lean production. Be innovative. Go global. Decentralize. TQM. Re-engineer. Brand yourself. Embrace e-commerce. Reorganize. Rethink teams. Strategically ally.*

Don't forget to be flexible! Monsanto's vision, for example, is sadly dilute: "operational excellence leading to a company that is flexible and responsive to an unpredictable business environment." Everyone knows that flexibility is good. When elevated to a vision, however, it gives free reign to avoid choices and hedge our bets. The faulty logic goes like this: "If we position ourselves as the best in something particular, customers might think we only do that. We might lose some other opportunity we don't know about yet."

Managing by the *bromide du jour* can send anyone into a tailspin. Worse, we often try to make all of them work at once, yielding a professional schizophrenia that makes us throw up our hands in misery. Lots of new employees, for example, are told that the company rewards those who are innovative, lean and mean, and make customers for life. Each of these qualities requires a certain temperament and set of behaviors. Ask any sole practitioner. Making personal relationships is not efficient, and lean production is rarely innovative. Be selective about management advice, and adopt the right set of strategies for your unique firm.

Assumption #4:
We're Problem-Solvers and Can Do Anything!
We're trained and educated as *problem-solvers*, a good foundation for any role in life. Although variety may offer spice, our clients don't see it that way at all when it comes to selecting their expert consultant.

In recent years, we've been through both a real estate depression and the vagaries of government programs, which together make for a survivalist mentality rather than an opportunity mentality. This gives rise to the industry joke, "How do you decide what jobs to chase?" Answer: "Anything that pays the rent!" (Not the recipe for wealth creation.)

The generalist/survivalist psychology harks back in part to the *Millionaire Next Door*. A surprising number of design professionals are children of these hearty self-made souls. As doting parents, they wish their offspring a better, easier life than the rough and tumble of their entrepreneurial one. To ensure this, they channel the next generation into the high-skill professions, where they are more insulated, and will enjoy higher prestige. This underlying dynamic structures an entire industry to be technically-driven and risk-averse.

Assumption #5:
Gotta Get Cheaper
Getting cheaper is a dead-end path. Even the manufacturing industry today has junked the adage, "lower your prices and make it up in volume." Low prices and high volume require a hard-nosed cost orientation which often results in an ant's-eye view, a riveting of attention on the tactical, operational, and financial. Like the proverbial traveling salesman, people are most concerned with "making the numbers" rather than being strategic. Utilization rates dominate the firm's thinking, while opportunities for fee leverage go begging. No wonder so many in our profession are exhausted.

Rather than ask the obvious question about getting cheaper, why not ask how the firm can make more money? What would happen if you challenge yourselves to achieve a 7.0 net multiplier instead of the usual 2.8 or 3.0? How would things change in the firm if each principal were to take home at least $350,000 per year in compensation? Try changing your perspective.

If being the low cost provider is truly a *strategic* goal of the firm, its business design and cost structure must be correct. This includes such components as locating the firm in low labor-cost areas like Greenville, South Carolina, composing the staff of a very few project managers and many paraprofessionals, offering more "productized" services, and outsourcing work to such places as India and China.

Assumption #6:
"Real Work" Means Doing Projects
Professionals, by definition, are highly trained in their work. The challenge of the project is the thing that they love, and it defines their personal satisfaction. They did not choose to become corporate executives. They did not begin their careers with management training programs like those provided at AT&T and IBM. They did not go to work for McKinsey or Arthur Andersen as a junior consultant.

Yet we expect outstanding business leadership abilities from people who think "real work" is being on the boards. Professionals spend years in school, work their way up to principal or owner, and are not about to throw it away for an administrative job.

Creating wealth, however, means viewing the design of the business as the *ultimate design challenge*. It is not enough to be the producer of a quality product.

The challenge is to forge a strong, vibrant enterprise composed of the right people, systems, and tools....which then produces the superb product.

Assumption #7:
At 50 We Can Start to Cruise
I'm always surprised by how many "52 year olds" want to retire early. As most of us get older, and into a more comfortable situation, we like change less and less. We've worked hard at our careers, and are looking for some security and some payback. Most of us want to avoid the pain of conflict. Risk is a drag. Drive is hard to come by.

But our 50s are prime leadership years. The successful leaders reach inside of themselves for new energy, often the energy of contribution. And contribution, whether to the community, to the industry, or to the body of professional knowledge, is a key element of the vigorous professional practice.

These seven assumptions set us up for generic and benign practices — practices so diluted that they have no edge, no foundation for success. Every day we see design professionals at a loss about how to prepare themselves for the future. They struggle for next-generation models for how to create themselves. Frankly, it's tough to see a different path from the way things have been, and it's tougher to have the courage to create something new and special.

We are not alone when we tenaciously cling to our old paradigms. American business at large is only now coming to grips with creating real strategy rather than simply operational efficiency. As an industry, we must

"Age makes you a conservative. The fact that you deserve it for all that hard work makes you a conservative."
Tom Peters

take the reins and show our business-world colleagues in other fields the courage to create truly rewarding practices.

In the following chapters, I'll make use of two essential concepts in creating wealth: the Wealth Equation, which explains the four prime principles, and the Sparks Framework, which describes the six key cultures and their business designs. As I discuss the four principles, I'll offer examples of how each type of firm in the industry actually applies the principles.

A brief preview is in order here.

THE WEALTH EQUATION

In our research for this book, we asked design firm leaders across the country to describe a situation in which they made their greatest profit. The answer we got is a simple one: *have something no one else has.* This is the fundamental organizing principle for creating wealth.

"Having something that no one else has," is indeed the heart of the matter. But to use the heart, you need a body too. You need special skills *and* an eager buyer to make the equation work.

The stories we heard from practitioners, many of whom suggested that they made two, three, or more times a typical consulting fee, all entailed both special expertise and a predisposed client. For example:

■ Rolf Jensen Associates exports its state-of-the-art fire protection technology to eager developing countries.

- Jaffe Holden Scarbrough Acoustics uses a high-tech "hearing dummy" to finely gauge design solutions for its noise-sensitive theater and automotive clients.
- G2 Architecture's Gerry Gerron cites the firm's extraordinary personal service to a select clientele of large commercial clients.
- Ambulatory care experts at Marshall Erdman offer a complete turn-key product to their clients, including fabrication of components in-house.
- ETS/PSI's systems help expedite the delivery of high volume telecommunications projects to its speed-driven clients.
- MK Centennial shares the risk on design/build projects with its "commodity-market" transportation clients.
- EDAW consultants analyze corporate clients' land holdings to show potential value in under-utilized properties.

The expert firms we researched also observed that once they had begun relationships with the right clients, they achieved an "insider position." The result: if the client was ever tempted to use another firm, they would endure a steep learning curve, the frustration of building new communication channels, and of course, lost time and money. Based on these unspoken consequences (and benefits), these firms continued to increase their fee leverage well above the norm for consulting. "We need you. Fee is not the issue," are the golden words.

Having something that no one else has, consists of four principles, or what we call The Wealth Equation. To achieve the "heart" expertise, you must be well-focused in a specific area of skill, and deliver a stream of new and better methods that advance this area of skill. To achieve the "body" of eager clients, you must target a specific, interested client base and provide for them a high level of credibility to gain their confidence. These four factors work together to yield an organization that creates wealth.

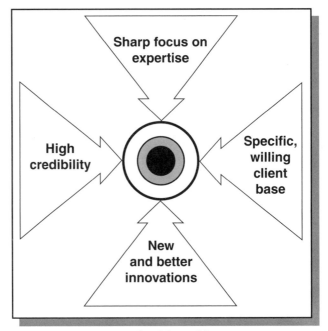

Four Principles of the Wealth Equation

If the firm fails to use these principles as an integrated whole, it will surely under-perform. Without focus, for example, the firm becomes diffuse and dilute. Without a willing client base, it experiences high costs and a low financial return. Without innovation, it is easily left behind the "better way" curve. And without credibility, it is not well recognized for its value. Do any of these describe your firm?

Even more dramatic are firms that rely on only one of the wealth principles. For example: Too much focus leads to an obsessive, introverted, technocratic culture that atrophies from lack of external influence. Too much reliance on the willing client base fosters eventual reactivity and loss of the leadership role. Too much innovation leads to the basement innovator syndrome, lacking attention to real-world delivery and marketing needs. And excessive dependence on credibility moves the firm toward a house of cards, an aging emeritus.

The only criteria of real importance are these: keep your eye on the ball of your substantive skill, be connected to a real and interested client base, continually strive for new and better ways of doing things, and exhibit credible proof of your contribution to the client.

THE SPARKS FRAMEWORK

The *Sparks Framework for Value Creation*™ is the model we have developed over years of working with design firms. What led us to develop the Sparks Framework was this: we found that most planning teams could manage the back-end planning well enough. They could extrapolate revenue, utilization, staff, and financial goals. They could tinker with ratios and sales targets. And they could create unending lists of tasks and action plans. But the front-end strategy, the crucial decisions about the firm's culture, distinction, and future direction, always proved daunting.

Although some firms were familiar with the Super Positioning Matrix, the industry's seminal strategy work

"We can evolve unconsciously without direction or we can evolve consciously and with choice. Either way, we evolve."
Gary Zukav
Seat of the Soul

developed by the Coxe Group, most still defaulted to hackneyed mission statements and vague wishes to be *"the premier firm in (blank), providing excellence in service and quality, and meeting or exceeding the client's expectations."* In other words, leaders of design firms plodded along as nice guys doing good work, but were unable to stand for something special in which to excel. They desperately needed an easily accessible, detailed road map of their possible choices – a clear way to decide their best direction, choose the right investments, and organize their firm for the future.

To fill the gap, we studied (and tried) many models for creating strategy, but our favorite was the framework created by Benjamin Tregoe and John W. Zimmerman in *Top Management Strategy: What It Is and How to Make It Work*. In essence, the authors outlined nine alternative driving forces that form the heart of differing corporations. We were also impressed with the clarity and accessibility of Swiss psychologist Carl Jung's six *Heroic Archetypes*.

Ultimately we developed our own six personality patterns for the design professions. They are:

- The Einsteins
- The Nichers
- The Market Partners
- The Community Leaders
- The Orchestrators
- The Builders

Each of these characters represents a distinct ecosystem. Each includes the underlying driving forces and core values that comprise its *culture*, as well as a scaffold of practices that comprise its *business design*.

Using our database of information on the top design firms, the Sparks Framework gives company leaders a technology for consciously designing their business. It's a test-drive simulator for decisions in marketing, human resources, finance, leadership, and project operations.

Before we go further, let's have a solid grounding in the economic dynamics that affect our practices.

CREATING WEALTH

Chapter Two

Wealth 101:
The Drivers
of the Economy

Even as our technologies change, the underlying principles of economics remain the same. In this section, we'll discuss four fundamental models that affect wealth creation in our firms. They are: supply and demand, the product life cycle, Porter's U-Curve, and value migration.

"It can be any size market but demand must be high and supply low. Therein lies the definition of value."

Tom Peters

SUPPLY AND DEMAND

Let's start the discussion with a basic definition of value: *"A product or service in high demand and low supply."*

What do you consider valuable? Recall what you were willing to pay for a gallon of gas in 1975. What about that sold-out Broncos jacket from the 1998 Super Bowl?

Have you ever needed a locksmith...right now? For something you really want, but can't get easily, you'd pay almost anything.

If you plot the curves of supply and demand in our industry, the picture that emerges is telling. Construction demand has its ups and downs, but overall is relatively stable. According to U.S. Department of Commerce statistics, the decade of 1986 to 1996 shows a negative 0.01 percent growth rate, while 1998 and 1999 show an all-time record of 3.0 percent. The long term projections for the next decade, however, show a slowdown to only 1.17 percent compound annual growth. Most of that growth is projected for residential construction, and technological advances such as telecommuting, electronic shopping, and teleconferencing will have a somewhat cooling effect on commercial building. Federal government spending is also predicted to drop.

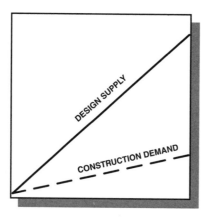

The supply and demand curves in the design industry show a disturbing trend that any practitioner can relate to on a gut level: an oversupply of professionals.

Let's match this with statistics in the design industry. Traditionally, design supply marginally exceeds construction demand. In the decade of 1986 to 1996, however, it generously exceeded demand, yielding the commodity markets that spawned aggressive price competition and bidding. As of this writing, demand is exceeding supply in many areas of the country, keeping fees healthy.

But in the decade ahead, three problematic factors will emerge: overoptimism, new entrants, and foreign competition. First, design firms are planning on a very rosy future. In fact, the design industry projects a 1.9 percent growth rate compared to a 1.1 percent growth rate projected for construction demand. Architects are particularly optimistic, projecting 2.4 percent growth. If they can recruit skilled people, and if school enrollments are any indication that they can, we should see another oversupply situation in the coming years.

Construction firms are entering the supply line, making headway in design/build and CM/PM work, and the accounting-consulting firms are already embedded in our industry. New foreign competition is well financed, and now easily accessible via cyberspace. The rest of the world is depending on exports to the U.S. for their own economic health.

The projected gap between the construction demand line and the AE supply line means trouble for the industry as a whole. This gap heralds a condition known as *high substitutability* in which the buyer has many choices with low perceived differences. In a buyer's market, the rational client seeks an equivalent product at the lowest price.

Robert Smith of the KPS Group conducted an analysis of fee trends by firms in the ENR 500. The surprising findings are consistent with the supply and demand graph.

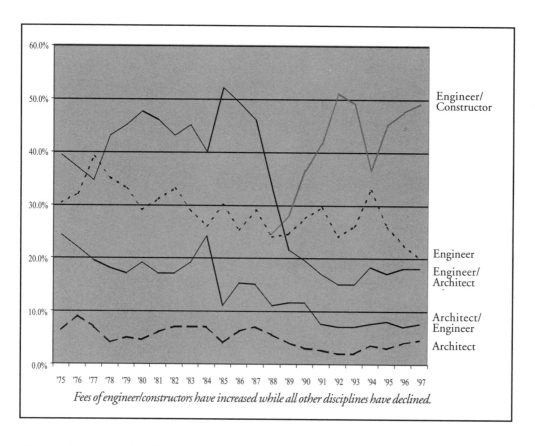

Fees of engineer/constructors have increased while all other disciplines have declined.

The study shows that between 1976 and 1998, billings per discipline changed as follows:

Billings by Discipline	1976	1998
Engineer	30.3%	20.2%
Engineer/architect	39.1%	18.2%
Architect/engineer	24.3%	7.7%
Architect	6.3%	4.7%
Engineer/constructor	N/A*	49.2%
	100.0%	100.0%

Percent tracked since 1989.

As a percent of the total pie, fees in each discipline have steadily declined, while fees in the engineering/construction sector, led by firms that excel at design/build, PM and CM are surging ahead. Design/build and PM are natural children of the supply and demand situation in which design professionals are so plentiful that the client can demand, and get, a quality project with a more tightly managed cost and schedule. According to some estimates, 50% of traditional work in the industry will be delivered in a design/build format by 2005. That's the game in a mature marketplace.

THE PRODUCT LIFE CYCLE

A major contribution to the understanding of marketplace dynamics, the product life cycle explains how products and markets behave. Fundamentally, markets experience a natural evolutionary momentum as they age, as do organizations, and of course, people themselves.

Let's examine laptop computers. In the early stages of the market, NEC and Zenith led the way with "portables." Demand was growing, but few products were available to serve the demand. As innovators, their job was to stimulate awareness, interest, and initial purchase – a process that takes time, but pays off in high prices. A few "early adopters" bought, especially those with a special problem or just a desire to be in the vanguard. This group typically provides a testing ground for the new offering.

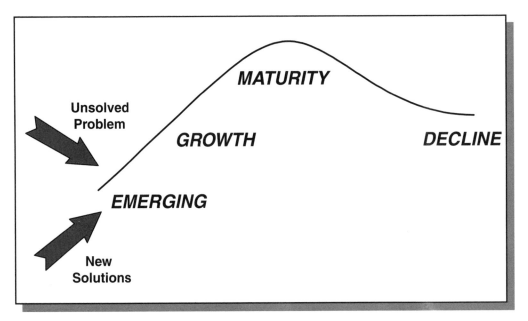

The product life cycle explains how products and markets behave.

If the product or service is satisfying, larger numbers of buyers are attracted and demand grows. Competitors such as Compaq and Toshiba entered the fray to help supply the need, and the adoption process began to take off. More buyers, the "early majority," entered as the service was legitimized, as did more suppliers – causing prices to fall. When demand and supply caught up with each other, IBM entered the market, just as Dell, Gateway, and Micron were capitalizing on the mature market.

Without a new curve, some things can disappear into mass market oblivion. Think how small accountants feel about Quicken, or residential contractors feel about Home Depot, or graphic designers feel about clip art.

Eventually new models emerge, which start new product curves. The evolution of battery technology, for example, opened a new generation of palm-tops.

Today, companies generate unlimited goods and services for virtually limitless needs. Demand is viewed in two ways, and both derive value from being "better." The first is *quantity* demand, in which price has high buyer influence, as in the commodity market. The second is *quality* demand, in which that "something special" has greater influence on the buyer.

Conveniently, the two types work in ascending waves in which quality items get less expensive as the market is saturated. Then the market is ready for something

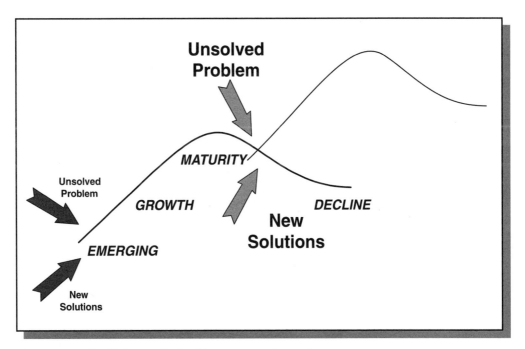

The new curve takes off when unsolved problems are met with new solutions.

else – a new, high priced product. That product then becomes more efficiently produced and the cycle continues. Program management is an example of high cost services today, evolved from the traditional general service package. Professional interior design is an example evolved from both architecture and interior "decoration" in the early 1960s. Sports facilities used to be considered basic, functional, nontechnical buildings until they were recast as a high-end specialty in the 1980s.

The study of paradigms tells us that a given solution can solve the problem reliably in 80% of the cases. But in the remaining 20%, the field is open for new solutions. This is where the new life cycle curve takes off. The length of the curves can vary, but the process remains the same.

James Rouse, founder of the Rouse Company, the nation's largest publicly held real estate development firm, worked for many years on the quantitative/mature side of the curve with his development business in low-end multifamily housing. In his later years, he invented high-end, blockbuster urban developments such as Underground Atlanta, Baltimore's Harbor Place, and Boston's Faneuil Hall that created a new, qualitative demand curve for the business. Today, we see a quantitative side explosion in "big box" retail centers, and an emerging qualitative demand for human scale Main Streets.

We can trace schools through the early days of Caudill Rowlett Scott and its new model featured in *Life Magazine* in the early '50s. A very special, very innovative product indeed, fit for the new generation. Today, however, many schools are built under commodity conditions with public advertisement and large numbers of qualified firms seeking selection. Wastewater treatment plants, roads and highways, and government offices are in the same condition. Perhaps they're ripe for a new wave?

Most of our firms operate on the well-trodden quantitative side where we know the rules. This puts us in a weak negotiating position – too many easy substitutes choking the pipeline.

THE U-CURVE OF MARKETPLACE EFFICIENCY

Harvard economist Michael Porter articulated one of the most compelling models for understanding the concept of expertise. In his books *Competitive Strategy* and *Competitive Advantage,* he correlates a company's volume and its profitability. The resulting U-shaped curve goes hand in hand with the two basic types of demand described above.

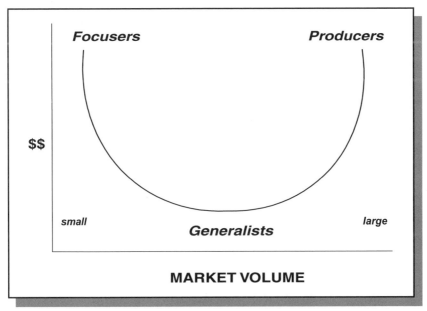

Those firms with clear expertise experience better financial results than generalists.

The curve shows the structurally weak *generalist* position compared with the focusers (qualitative) and producers (quantitative). In other words, those who make the highest financial returns are clearly differentiated in some way, either through brains or brawn. Both yield efficiencies. Thus the focuser and the producer offer two fundamental ways to differentiate services and provide value. There are many other ways, but these two methods suggest a good starting point.

One of our clients dubbed the U-Curve the "bathtub" and it stuck. In other words, if you see yourself where many practitioners do – at the bottom of the curve – you're probably taking a bath. Porter's concept was fundamental in our understanding of focus, and in the early development of the Sparks Framework.

Many practitioners grew up with a broad-brush perspective on practice, beginning their careers in full-service local firms. Compound this mindset with educators' valid mandate to teach broad-based process skills, and you've got a scenario that would make a generalist out of anyone.

Were you taught that as a professional you were a free-ranging *problem-solver*? We've had clients actually suggest that problem-solving is their distinctive edge (while their accountant, marketing director, and lawyer sat in the room wondering if *they* weren't problem-solvers!). Fact is, nature gives every human being the ability to solve problems.

Some generalists claim they bring a "fresh approach." What they say is true, but it's the rare client who buys that way today. It just doesn't make sense to send a firm to school "on us."

Generalists have a *survivalist* mindset, for good reasons:

- They can't create enough value in the marketplace to invest sufficiently in the skills that create efficiencies.

- They lose out on good work because they can't show depth of experience.

- Their work quality is poor because they're inexperienced in the specifics of the problem.

- They rarely make money because their value is not perceived or they don't know the short cuts.

- Their corporate culture is blurry, with conflicting internal messages.

- Their resources are diluted on a wide variety of investments which yield low returns.

When asked to describe himself, the clever generalist first asks the client, "What do you need?" His answer: "Interesting, that's just what we do!" He sings the praises of his firm's diversification, but their SF255 and similar projects lists tell a weak story.

The weakest performers are the generalists. In other words, being *an inch deep and a mile wide* is not a selling point in today's market. Generalist firms are competitively disadvantaged in both specialized experience and in cost/time efficiencies.

As they say in Texas, "the only thing in the middle of the road is a yellow line and a dead armadillo."

In a global economy, clients want and can get experts for their important projects. Where speed is an issue, the great project managers prevail. Where prestige is an issue, the cutting-edge designer prevails. Where politics is an issue, the locally connected firm prevails.

Both the focuser and producer capitalize on a carefully crafted set of strategies and practices to sustain their expertise. The focuser beats the generalist on value added, and the producer beats the generalist on value saved. With our clients, we've seen upwards of 50% net profit for the "brains" side, and up to 20% net profit for the "brawn" side.

To excel, firms need an *opportunity* mindset in order to develop strong competitive strategy. Generalists have the opposite: a *survivalist* mindset.

Value Migration

When were your theories of business molded? Plenty of today's leaders came of age in the good ol' days and continue to live there mentally.

Although our material goods were much fewer, and many jobs were mundane, no one can deny that the post-World War II '50s, '60s, and early '70s in the U.S. were unprecedented expansion years. The baby boom generation was birthed and the suburbs were developed. The Great Society provided plenty of momentum for schools, interstate highways, and manufacturing.

Most of today's largest design and construction firms were formed during this period. They grew rapidly, thanks to our country's driving need for infrastructure, housing, and consumer goods. For firms of this era, it was clearly sensible to operate on as large a scale as possible, to serve the needs of the exploding population. This is where our mindset of "bigger is better" was formed.

The changes we've observed over the last few decades, and how these will play out in the decade ahead, can best be seen when we look out over the years at such dimensions as the buyer-seller relationship, markets and marketing, customer loyalty, and organizational values. Notice how each era assigns value differently, and how today's value is migrating to the experts.

The Post-War Expansion Era: In the post-war period, the producer was king. Consumers wanted whatever could be produced, and more – houses, cars, appliances, etc. Firms were well organized, under control by the hierarchy, and customers were loyal to the brand. Alfred Sloan of GM invented the ingenious automotive ladder – "a car for every purse and purpose." As you progressed in your career, you came in with a Chevrolet, moved through to the Pontiac, Olds, Buick, and on up to the Cadillac. Just as we always used Pepsodent and smoked Kents, the old boy network of relationships was sacred: "We've used Bob for 30 years on all our hospital work." Firms like HOK, SOM, Bechtel, and CH2MHill were established and grew to huge size.

	'50s '60s '70s Expansion	'80s '90s Commodity	2000 + Leadership
Who's King:	Producer	Customer	Expert
Market:	Mass market	Fragmented market	Net markets
Marketing:	Generalist, old school marketing	Mass marketing advertising	Positioning, Public Relations
Customer Loyalty:	Brand loyalty	Self-loyalty	Collaborative
Organizational Values:	Sturdy, stable, hierarchical	Productivity, efficiencies	Nimble, creative, teams

The Commodity Market Era: Our growth slowed in the '80s and '90s, and almost all of our businesses and institutions saw a dramatic change from producer-as-king to customer-as-king. *Supply exceeded demand*, and the commodity market flourished. Marketing became essential, and the Society for Marketing Professional Services was born. Customer loyalty was moving out, and self-loyalty was moving in. Bob was out of luck if somebody else offered a better deal, a smarter idea, or the promise of greater speed. Everyone struggled to get lean and mean, in order to provide the cost and speed edge. Everyone tried to differentiate by "service and quality," but these soon turned into *prerequisites* rather than differentiators.

<u>The Leadership Era</u>: The millennium is the era of the focused expert. In the next decade, we expect that our research will bear out: It's not just "listening" that clients want. Some 96 percent want a professional suited exactly to their problem area, whether technical, price, or process-oriented.

Count on the expert firm to link with a network of other expert partners to provide the total package that best fits a given client's needs. Several consultants are already in business to broker these teams and networks, and the technology for team-based web sites and virtual organizations is here. Expect networks to be three-dimensional including the traditional design disciplines as well as specialty disciplines such as lawyers, real-estate developers, futurists, contractors, and in some cases, even clients themselves.

The requirements of the leadership era can be tough, especially for the current "command generation." Ideally, these individuals are energetic role models and champions. But, in practice, many in their 50s and 60s have achieved their career goals and now lack personal drive. It takes real commitment to turn a ship that is comfortable operating within an established, if less-than-effective, system. And it takes real commitment to stand out, to seek distinction. But seek distinction we must. Why?

- Because industry supply and demand form a commodity picture;
- Because the product life cycle curve will sweep us toward maturity;
- Because the focusers and producers reap the highest return on their efforts; and,
- Because value has migrated to the experts.

"The two most valuable ideas in the old economic order: market share and growth, have become the two most dangerous ideas in the new order."

Adrian Slywotzky and David Morrison
The Profit Zone: How Strategic Business Design Will Lead You to Tomorrow's Profits

45

Most firms will never have the resources of our industry's hallowed mega-firms. But most won't have the baggage either. So why not assume a leadership role for the millennium? As Will Rogers said, "You have to go out on a limb – that's where the fruit is!"

Chapter Three

Creating Wealth
Principle One:

Clarity of Focus

Focus is the most elemental principle of wealth creation. Simply put, if we want to be considered valuable, we must become something special, something rare. The minute we start hedging our bets is the minute we lose focus, and thus our value-producing potential.

"We invest in highly focused, one-of-a-kind businesses."
Warren Buffett
Chairman,
Berkshire Hathaway
Multi-billionaire

JOB #1 IN THE
WORLD OF CONSUMER PRODUCTS

In the product world, the *good fight* is about counteracting commoditization. Manufacturers understand what high substitutability does to pricing, and they take action. They embrace the reality of a focused, differentiated position in the marketplace and use it to their advantage. They also elevate clever marketing minds to the highest levels.

As you read the business press and consume everyday products, notice the power of well-focused companies and your mental connection with their names. Who comes to mind when you think about:

- The most reliable overnight shipping?
- The most advanced microprocessor chips?
- Lowest price airfares?
- The ultimate driving machine?
- The world class US music school?
- Mail order computers?

Did you think right away of FedEx, Intel, Southwest, BMW, Julliard, and Dell? They are great examples of focus. Focus applies to people and places too.

FOCUS E X A M P L E S

Excellence	Tom Peters
Paradigms	Joel Barker
Marriage counseling	Dr. Ruth
Muscle men	Arnold Schwarzenegger
Consumer electronics	Japan
Vodka and caviar	Russia
Private international banking	Switzerland
Computer development	Silicon Valley
Diamonds	South Africa
Country music	Branson, Missouri (with 40 music halls, now threatening Nashville!)

The definitive work on the subject is *Focus: the Future of Your Company Depends on It*, by Al Ries. In his book, Ries cites hundreds of examples of success gained by focusing as well as failures due to rampant growth and diversification mania.

One of the most dramatic stories is GE, the company that *Forbes* rates the world's most valuable long-term corporation. When Jack Welch took the role of CEO, he began by cutting one-half of GE's staff and whittling down 44 businesses to yield the top 12. Then he formulated a depth-oriented service and consulting strategy as well as a CEO-to-CEO marketing strategy for each division. These moves renewed GE's value, and paid off handsomely.

The strongest players of tomorrow will be sharply focused on the client base *that they define and choose to capture*. Because of this focus, they will foresee market shifts and evolving client needs well ahead of the pack. They will be innovating ways to improve their work and their clients' success. And they will prove highly resistant to competition. This formula does not require that the firm achieve huge size and volume, although it may be a necessity for some.

> *"You have to have a focus. A focus implies a narrowing of the business with the intent to dominate a segment. There's power when you can own a market. There's no power when you're a bit player."*
>
> Al Ries
> *Focus: the Future of Your Company Depends on It*

SUCCESS STORIES IN THE DESIGN PROFESSIONS

An (anonymous) representative from the Corps of Engineers Medical Group confided to us recently that they only hire the "real experts in health care." If an architect or engineer doesn't have "extensive health care experience," he said, "no amount of relationship, service, or price will help. These days there are so many A/Es," he continued, "you can just go down to the corner and flag one down!"

The ideal condition is to *own a position in the client's mind.* You want the client to say, "Hmmm, we have a really important bridge project, and need an expert. Clearly, this is the firm of choice. They are the pros!" The path to wealth is paved with easy identification and mental preference. It's about being something special.

In our consulting practice, we are constantly polling design professionals as well as owners in the public and private sectors about "who's who" among design firms. Here is a brief sampling of those perceptions. (This list is not intended to be inclusive, just some examples. Note also that we've selected highly visible firms for the purposes of clarity. There are many others with smaller practices that dominate their geographic and specialty markets, but wouldn't be widely known to all readers.)

FOCUS EXAMPLES

Airports	HNTB, Parsons, URS/Greiner
Stadiums	HOK Sport, Ellerbe Becket, NBBJ
Sustainable Design	William McDonough, Croxton Collaborative
Resorts	Wimberly Allison Tong & Goo
Design-Build	Bechtel, Fluor Daniel, The Austin Company
Bridges	Parsons Brinckerhoff, Figg, T.Y. Lin
Hazardous Waste	CH2MHill, Raytheon, EarthTech
Land Planning	Sasaki, EDAW, SWA Group
Signature Buildings	Frank Gehry, Renzo Piano, Rem Koolhaus

Each of these firms has something in common. Somewhere along the line, they recognized an opportunity. They committed to being the best in their chosen specialty, and invested real resources in it. They disciplined themselves to hire the right staff, market the right clients, and create project delivery systems that are right for their expertise. In short, they focused and built a leadership position. None of this happened by luck, but by sheer vision, passion, and doggedness. These firms will continue their record success, if they keep their eye on the ball.

THE DIVERSIFICATION TRAP

"There is only one rung on the ladder in the client's mind that you can occupy," say Trout and Ries, the authors of *Positioning: The Battle for Your Mind,* one of the seminal works in corporate strategy. Those who get there first with a new development not only raise the bar, but establish a strong leadership role. They tend to stay in the leadership position and enjoy the benefits.

"Man who chases two rabbits catches neither."

Confucius

Most industry CEOs recognize that their essential role is to lead their company into the future. Unfortunately, these same CEOs interpret this mandate as getting into new markets, services, and geographies. In the majority of cases, this is defensive, nonstrategic thinking. Why?

The first problem is that the CEO fails to recognize the likelihood of someone else holding a leadership role in these "new" areas already. The second problem is that in its eagerness to define and enter new markets, the firm dilutes its limited resources across several fronts at once, guaranteeing a weak performance. The third problem is that it lets the firm avoid experimenting within its existing area of strength, and ultimately building mastery through innovation. An interesting example of building mastery through innovation can be seen in Sir Norman Foster and Partners, a London-based firm that takes its structurally inspired architecture into the design of structural products. The bridge from innovation to offering is what creating wealth is about.

Just imagine members of a medical practice saying this to themselves: "We're known as terrific brain surgeons, so let's get into prosthesis insurance, and diagnostic software. They're hot new trends." It *never* happens in medicine.

Nothing is inherently wrong with exploring new markets and services. In fact, this kind of exploration may be necessary under well-defined circumstances, such as

Here are the three best reasons to avoid diversification:

1. Your image becomes diffuse, and the client can't identify your distinctive expertise;

2. Your resources are split among a variety of initiatives, all of which benefit halfway;

3. Your leaders lack the management drive and skills to effectively optimize diverse operations.

escaping a client base that is less than satisfying. But taken as a mandate for the CEO job description, this preoccupation with diversification rather than depth and innovation will lead to the dilution of focused expertise, and eventually the erosion of the firm's value.

If you're still doubting, consider how focus works in other nonbusiness dimensions of our lives. For example, society prefers us to have only one spouse. Although trying at times, this focus yields a better biological result in the survival and success of offspring. Consider the mantra of the military mind – "deep penetration on a narrow front." Consider how important pruning is to a healthy garden. Consider the practice time great golfers, skiers, or tennis players invest in their game. Compared to the weekend athlete, their focus rewards them with a fine living.

Our practices are just the same.

SPARKS CULTURAL ARCHETYPES AND THEIR DRIVING FORCES

Remember the famous scene in *City Slickers*?

> *"Do you know what the secret to life is?" asks Jack Palance.*
>
> *"No, what?" says Billy Crystal.*
>
> *"One thing, just one thing. You stick to that and everything else don't mean shit."*
>
> *"That's great, but what's the one thing?"*
>
> *"That's what you've got to figure out."*

In the seventeenth century, famed scientist Robert Hooke was known for his contributions in physics, astronomy, chemistry, biology, geology, architecture, paleontology, and naval technology. There was a lot less information in those days!

By contrast, I was on a selection panel to recommend a certification consultant for the Society for Marketing Professional Services. Of the many competitors, several were testing consultants with personal names, e.g. Brown & Associates. One was named Professional Examination Services. And one poor soul was a generalist consultant who offered certification, recruiting, marketing plans, strategic planning, and a host of other services. We immediately disqualified the last entry, somehow knowing he couldn't be that good. The personal names were neutral. But of all the proposals on the table, whose voice was clear and strong? The expert – the name confirmed it, and so did their well-designed business.

The Sparks Framework for Value Creation offers a good starting place for making that "one thing" decision, the most important decision you can make in company strategy.

The Sparks model outlines six cultural patterns representing specific value-generating business designs. Each has a unique operating model that reinforces its distinctive expertise.

Each culture is fundamentally created around a driving force – an energized value system that forms the organizing principle of the firm. Driving forces can be discovered by looking at who the firm hires, promotes, and rewards, as well as its chosen client base. What behavior is most valued?

The following chart illustrates the six cultural patterns and their driving forces. The range of choices is wide, but again the trick is to truly master one.

CULTURES	D R I V I N G F O R C E S
Einstein	Invention of new theories and technologies
Niche Expert	Advancement of the niche through application of the latest ideas
Market Partner	Securing lifelong client relationships through immersion in a mutually-shared market type
Community Leader	Securing lifelong client relationships through immersion in a mutually-shared commitment to community betterment
Orchestrator	Achieving dominion over project complexity
Builder	Saving the client time and money while delivering a quality product

■ *The Einstein firm* is built around the generation of original ideas and new technologies. In architecture, they are the high-profile design firms with original styles or philosophies. In engineering, they're the PhDs with strong research and development functions. Einsteins work with research grants or endowments, and staff members love to experiment as well as teach and publish. Einsteins are known for a distinctive set of original ideas, and can apply them across building types and geographies. Their philosophy, however, is singularly focused.

Examples are Frank Gehry, Santiago Calatrava, Michel Virlogeux, and Buckminster Fuller. Einstein firms also include Pixar, Dreamworks, Eye Candy and other computer entertainment companies (that are recruiting top design graduates from MIT and other prestigious universities, and paying six-figure salaries).

■ *Niche Experts* are dedicated to a specific project-type or service-type within a broader market. They watch the experiments of the Einsteins, and adapt them to create state-of-the-art work. They frequently team through a network of other firms to provide full services for a given project, and are often national or international in scope.

HOK Sport is a *project-type* nicher. Besides its highly acclaimed focus on sports facilities, HOK Sport enjoys a unique, uncompromised reputation relative to its parent company, HOK. It benefits from a separate, descriptive name, a separate location, and separate management. What's even more interesting is that it has micro-niches: NHL/NBA arenas, collegiate and minor league arenas, olympic arenas, major league ballparks, training ballparks, collegiate ballparks, minor league ballparks, NFL stadiums, collegiate stadiums, rugby/soccer stadiums, and university recreation centers. The market recognizes HOK Sport internationally. Few others in the design profession can boast a cover story in *USA Today*!

Duany Plater-Zyberk is a *service-type* nicher focusing on new urbanism master planning. Andres Duany and Elizabeth Plater-Zyberk have built a marketplace powerhouse commanding some of the highest fees in the profession. Wiss Janney Elstner is known for its building technology forensic work, Cini-Little is known for food service, Rolf Jensen leads the market in fire protection, Weidlinger is called in worldwide for blast-related issues, Walter P. Moore excels in sports and convention center structures as well as public assembly structures, and Allan Greenberg specializes in neoclassical architecture.

Besides the project and service-types, niches can also be grown around themes or issues, such as energy-efficiency, fund-raising, and public consensus-building.

■ *Market Partners* lead in one or a few major markets such as health care and transportation. They recognize, and choose to be part of, a distinct client world. Montgomery Watson and CDM are Market Partners committed to the water and wastewater markets. Shepley Bulfinch Richardson and Abbott is a Market Partner committed to the "learning" market. ADP Marshall is committed to the microelectronics/lab/R&D market.

Market Partners are strong advocates for their clients as well as the client industry, often leading lobbying efforts and crusading at trade meetings. They enjoy a number of patrons with whom they share the same goals and values, creating a base of personal friendships. Market partners typically serve multiple segments within their industry, and benefit from offering a broad range of services to support their chosen market (and keep them coming back for more).

"A point of view adds at least 80 points to your I.Q."
Marvin Minsky
Pioneering Scientist in
Artificial Intelligence

Another strategy typical of the Market Partner is to incorporate former client-side staffers into the firm. Ai, an architecture, engineering, and interior design firm focused on the corporate market, gains legitimacy from Rusty Meadows' AT&T background. General Sverdrup used his client-side experience in building McArthur's airfields in the Pacific, and Missouri Highway Department's roads and bridges to leverage his transportation-based engineering enterprise. Firms keyed to the federal markets have former employees of the target agencies in high level marketing or project management positions. This represents a significant dedication to the market of choice.

■ *Community Leaders* aim for a leadership role in their town's action. They sink deep roots into the community, developing close relationships on both a social and political level. They seek the premier local project work, which ranges across the board in size and type, including public buildings, police and fire stations, recreation centers, schools, shelters, public works, and other municipal facilities. For those projects requiring significant technical knowledge, they team with a network of Niche Experts around the country.

Many design professionals begin with a small, local practice. The difference, however, between being a high performing Community Leader and an under-performing generalist, is that Community Leaders are so woven into the fabric of the community that they open doors that are closed to outsiders. They can expedite decision-making by virtue of their professional and personal relationships in the community.

One of the best examples of a Community Leader is Carde Ten Architects in Santa Monica, California. Focused on municipal work, the firm packages entire projects for its *potential* clients, including scouting real estate deals and securing funding. This "risky" behavior is mitigated because they know their community so well. Result: staff members enjoy doing good design, but no longer struggle with the typical design firm's fee-for-time treadmill.

Community Leaders invest heavily in their local networks. Freidl Bohm, president of NBBJ, established his infrastructure in Columbus, Ohio with the Young Presidents Organization, local board involvement, and ownership in a successful chain of restaurants in town. Harvey Gantt served as mayor of Charlotte, North Carolina, again illustrating a depth of commitment to the community.

■ *The Orchestrator* is focused on outstanding project management, bringing its skills to bear on large, complex projects, including the best design/build jobs. Emphasis is on speed, coordination, and control. Many Orchestrators are known for their PM/CM expertise. Some are even called "management consultants," like the team of Bechtel and Parsons Brinckerhoff on the mammoth Central Artery Tunnel project in Boston.

Bechtel, Fluor Daniel, and the engineer/constructors are classic Orchestrators. The leading program managers, such as Heery International, 3D/International, and Sverdrup CRSS are Orchestrators.

In some A/E circles, practitioners bemoan the fact that the big accounting firms, including Ernst & Young, and Andersen Consulting are moving onto our turf. In fact, they are taking advantage of a high-demand Orchestrator role. You won't see them active in the other archetype patterns.

Askew Nixon Ferguson is an example of a smaller firm operating as an Orchestrator. Early in its history, ANFA started out working for Federal Express, by definition a speed and logistics-oriented client. The firm developed a culture to match, full of high-energy people concerned with good project management. Today ANFA is still working for Federal Express, but has added other fast-paced project types, such as casinos.

Privatization is the realm of the Orchestrator. Because Orchestrators know their process, and enjoy logistical challenges, they work effectively on these financial/technical behemoths. Of all the archetypes, this is where we find the lion's share of MBAs.

■ *The Builder* has the real cost advantage, focusing on prototypes, site adaptations, and multi-site project rollouts for retail stores, HMOs, branch banks, service stations, telecommunications towers, U.S. Job Corp centers, and mass government office space.

Volume rollouts, a fast and inexpensive way for client organizations to expand into multiple geographic markets, save the costs of individually developed and designed units. Tulsa-based BSW International is a leader here, specializing in "multiple-facility building programs" for clients such as Wal-Mart, Circuit City, and Marriott. BSW is unabashedly dedicated to improving its clients' financial success, and even casts itself as a real estate development services company that offers program management, real estate and site development services as well as design and construction. The firm has been featured in *Wall Street Journal, Business Week, Inc., Fortune,* and *PC Today* as a thriving example not only in the design industry, but also as a leader among American service firms.

Black & Veatch is another top Builder. A major engineering/construction firm, its production center in Kansas City, Missouri allows staff to execute the work in an extremely efficient manner. This edge helps it to dominate many markets, to reap the benefits of high volume, and to extend itself internationally – at a lower risk than those who struggle to produce a consistently reliable work product.

Interestingly, Builders have been successful with total quality management, unlike other firms in the profession that view speed and cost leadership as unprofessional. Because Builders are such an integral part of their client's financial success, they move very quickly. And if you're committed to beating the budget and schedule, you need a serious program that assures quality – just like your clients have.

In selecting their driving force and culture, firm leaders often ask us if they can (please!) span multiple types. The answer: being seated in one type is easier on the organization – you know exactly what your culture demands when recruiting and promoting people, managing ownership succession, and a host of other issues arise.

Most firms, however, choose some type of hybrid arrangement. Recall the product life cycle curve and the forward momentum that flows along the curve as entities evolve. Linking this idea with the six cultural archetypes, you can see that the Einsteins exist in the emergence zone of the curve, the Niche Experts in the growth zone, the Market Partners and Community Leaders in the stability zones, and the Orchestrators and Builders in the maturity zones (see graph on p. 90).

Most firm leaders will strive to maintain their culture of choice by *placing an upstream anchor in the flowing river* that is the curve. This means that Market Partners will select a few good niches, Orchestrators will anchor in a specific community, Nichers will nurture a few experimental projects, and so on. Since these upstream components are fundamentally different cultures than the firm itself, a struggle will always exist.

Someone at the top must actively protect these atypical ventures. For example, Howard Noel, chairman of Virginia-based A/E firm Hayes Seay Mattern & Mattern, is focused on the *Market Partner* firm's upstream niche, watershed management. Larry Plunkett, president of the national design/build *Orchestrator* firm, Sachs Electric, is focused on their upstream home-base community of St. Louis. Tom Livingston, president of the Alaska *Community Leader,* Livingston Slone, focuses on the upstream market, cultural facilities.

For more on the six cultures, please refer to *The Sparks Framework: A Handbook of Value-Creation Strategies,* and its companion self-assessment, *The Sparks Framework Assessment: Charting Your Preferences.*

TAPPING INTO THE PASSIONATE INTEREST

Now that you have a feel for the six cultural patterns, turn to your firm and identify its leaders' and stakeholders' most passionate interest. This is the wellspring of success. Sparks fly when your expertise is the reflection of your passion.

Your firm's passionate interest sets the pace for the character of your organization. When the focus is shared, you release a vibrancy that energizes the firm and can't help but attract clients. Imagine a passion for creating the best senior living facilities in the world. Everything the firm does revolves around advancing this expertise: choosing staff, marketing, offering stock, and designing your office, not to mention defining your project technologies.

As a senior living Niche Expert, for example, you devote yourself to advancing your state-of-the-art work. But you also research the latest experiments from around the world, keep up with the Market Partners in the health care industry, monitor local regulations and demographics, and hone your project management skills.

"Although we're most essentially a design firm, Cesar Pelli & Associates is extremely responsible about our client's budget, schedule, program, and site. In fact, we view these design constraints as critical parameters of our creative work"
Phillip G. Bernstein
Cesar Pelli & Associates

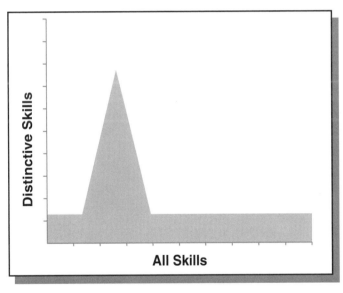

All firms need a solid baseline of skills as well as one thing they do superbly.

Whatever your driving force, you needn't forsake the other qualities that are required for successful project work. In fact, you *must* offer competent and responsible skills in client relationships, cost and schedule control, and quality of work.

The key to a wealth-creating firm is that you select *something* and build it to a high level of distinction. Fortunately, there are many ways to be an expert, not to mention clever combinations.

WEALTH BUILDERS:

1. Rivet their attention on their driving force and its opportunities,

2. Soundly reject the marginal temptations of "hot" new markets, and

3. Seize resources to strengthen the organization with the right staff, projects, and clients.

Wealth builders are confident. They know who they are, and they stand for something. They are persistent and committed.

Chapter Four

Creating Wealth
Principle Two:

The Willing Client Base

Profit comes from customers. And only one thing really matters to clients: they MUST reduce their risk and maximize their return. To the extent that they can, they'll hire the best in whatever it is that they perceive they need.

In our focus groups, owners tell us they want their design professionals to guide them and advise them – to *lead them* in their project, or at least be their trusted equal. Whenever consultants get into a situation where they're considered technocrats, or worse, an "extra pair of hands," they lose leverage and respect. Manpower is easier to obtain than talent, and doesn't cost much. Wealth creators stay ahead of the client, providing leadership, confidence, and valuable results.

"Value migrates toward activities that are most important to the customer."
Adrian Slywotzky
Value Migration: How to Think Several Moves Ahead of Competition

THE MATCH GAME

In the vast network that is the marketplace, there are as many kinds of clients as stars in the sky. What's required of you as a wealth-builder is to figure out exactly which client base will allow you to create the highest profit within your area of passion. The analysis begins with these three questions:

1. *Who needs us?*
2. *What are their most critical problems?*
3. *For what service will they pay the highest fees?*

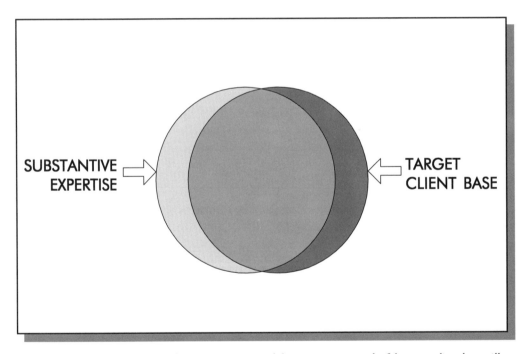

The degree of overlap of the firm's substantive expertise and the most pressing needs of the target client base will determine value perceived and realized.

If their problem is getting through city hall, they'll look for an expert in local connections – a Community Leader. If their problem is a complex project with a killer schedule, they'll look for an expert in logistics – an Orchestrator. If they need to elevate their image to attract a national audience or big-time investor, they'll need an Einstein.

Whatever the client's need, the best matching firm will save the client time and reduce the client's risk. (Imagine how much longer it would take Black & Veatch as opposed to Cesar Pelli to design a high-profile office tower in Singapore. Imagine how much riskier it would be to rely on London-based Ove Arup and Partners as opposed to Alexandria Surveys to get through Alexandria's permitting department.)

The business literature touts monolithic markets: the construction market, the schools market, the water market, the transportation market. In fact, there are many ways to define markets. A better way to define the market for any particular firm is to identify the client base by its predominant needs.

For example, structural engineers Thornton-Thomasetti, with a portfolio that includes United Airlines at O'Hare, the Petronas Towers in Kuala Lumpur, and the New York Hospital Expansion over FDR Drive in New York City, looks for projects "that everyone else is afraid of." They clearly seek opportunities to innovate.

Thornton-Thomasetti's client base has a substantially different agenda than Denver architects Pahl, Pahl, and Pahl, whose client base includes LaQuinta Inns, Hampton Inns, and Homewood Suites. Both firms have a willing market and a client base that will pay for the

"Know thyself, know thy client, and know thy enemy."
Guy Kawasaki
How to Drive the Competition Crazy

special expertise they bring. *The key is to match your most distinctive expertise with your targeted client base — and its agenda.*

THE CLIENT'S AGENDA

Using the Sparks Framework, we can describe six typical client patterns and their most characteristic needs. This stands in sharp contrast to the conventional business advice that most clients want one-stop-shopping or its equivalent, a full array of "non-traditional services." The point is this: There are no single correct strategies, no one-size-fits-all. You must select your client base according to your firm's driving force, and then deeply understand its constituents.

■ *Einstein Clients* need a cutting-edge image, often to attract the best of its target customers: top law students, big investors, economic development prospects, and important conventions. Sometimes Einstein clients suffer from "esteem" issues; they need to counteract a boring, overly-conservative image. Even cities fall into this category. For example, Columbus, Ohio used avant-garde architect Peter Eisenman for its convention center. Likewise, Pittsburgh shortlisted Vignoli, Pelli, Arquitectonica, and Skidmore Owings and Merrill.

The Einstein client can be found in academia, civic life, corporate life, or public life, but always seeks a statement designer or a research-based engineer. On their cutting-edge water facilities, for example, cities might choose a firm like Carollo Engineers, with its dedicated R&D group of PhDs doing research in membrane technology and other experimental areas.

Most Einstein clients look for a national or international reputation to enhance their team, as do the Niche Expert clients (below).

CULTURES CLIENT AGENDA

Einstein Client	Needs to fulfill need for prestige, improved image
Niche Expert Client	Needs to overcome risky, adverse conditions
Market Partner Client	Needs to augment client's own skills, as full services "partner"
Community Leader Client	Needs facilitation through community gatekeepers
Orchestrator Client	Needs to control project complexity
Builder Client	Needs to deliver the product, optimizing the budget

■ *Niche Expert Clients* need to counter either an unusual, high-risk situation or objections from some party to the project. To accomplish these goals, this client needs an expert in the specific specialty area to overcome resistance and increase confidence. Perhaps a given city needs to create a new comprehensive plan, but it suffers from a poor track record for public consensus. Any mistakes will cause the city's leadership to take the blame. They need a proven firm, so they choose one that is nationally known for consensus-building skills, such as American Communities Partnership.

Perhaps the challenge is a new, high-density urban development that's fraught with angry citizens and development issues. The client might choose Duany Plater-Zyberk to build a compelling design with citizen and developer input. William McDonough, specializing in environmentally-oriented design, collaborated with Gensler, a Market Partner, to deliver a new headquarters for the Gap. This kind of "green" statement, if done well, plays well with shareholders. If done poorly, it can look like a waste of shareholder equity, and generate waves on the stock market. Higher risk calls for specific expertise.

■ *Market Partner Clients* need a trusted partner to get a variety of projects completed – not a guru and not a production firm, but a firm that can integrate in broad-reaching ways into the client's organization. A firm that, if the client could clone himself, he would own. Key managers and staff would look like him, talk like him, be concerned with the same issues, and know the same people. In short, this client needs "partners" who know how things really work in the industry.

Art Gensler, founder of one of the great Market Partner firms, was once characterized as being "as highly respected by his competitors as he is by the clients whose corporations he may understand *better* than they do." According to Gensler, "We've got 30 business consultants helping clients with workplace strategy, getting us involved earlier in the process as well as after the project is complete. Our teams are involved with branding through asset management."

■ *Community Leader Clients* need a firm that is a competent provider of design services, but more importantly contains people who know how to get things done in town: people who know the right people to expedite the project, either from a political/bureaucratic standpoint, or from a social standpoint. Bottom line: the client's problems are about moving the project through approvals and gaining local user acceptance.

The typical client may be a city or state agency whose leaders are motivated by a political or taxpayer preference. It may be a locally-based enterprise, or a national enterprise seeking to burrow into the local economy. This works similarly in the social context. Consider the landscape designer who designs the estates of the rich and famous in the area. The firm is active in fundraisers, which facilitates social approval and acceptance. Its principals host evenings in their own experimental gardens, and they may even do a radio call-in show about planting design.

If your firm is a known contributor to the community, you're likely to have a cachepot of good will among both obvious and hidden project gatekeepers. Your clients will recognize this value.

■ *Orchestrator Clients* have a huge project to manage, with multiple sites and multiple teams, and little internal capability. In short, they need a virtual facilities department to act on their behalf to implement the job. For example, the Dallas Independent School District won a $275 million bond for a new facilities program, and it selected Heery International as program manager. Heery then mobilized staffing, organized minority business involvement, created budgets, coordinated the hiring of design firms, oversaw construction documents, selected contractors, and followed through after completion.

The critical problem for the client is project management; it matters little whether it is delivered in a program management, CM-at-risk, or design/build format.

■ *Builder Clients* need the approved facility built in multiple locations, at top speed and at best price. This often involves a prototype, which is developed either by the firm, by another firm, in-house, or in some combination. The client's problem is getting the job done in the most efficient manner possible, at the best cost, with acceptable quality. They're not looking for ego in a design firm.

This is the land of facility rollouts, including branch banks, service station convenience store conversions, chain hotels, big-box retail facilities, and franchises. The use of prototypes and site adaptations even extends to cash-strapped school districts in North Carolina and Florida. For these demanding projects, clients need a firm with excellent production skills and technologies. This type of client and its mate, the Builder, can often do very well with incentive fees, in which both sides can win big.

From this discussion, you can see the key concept, creating wealth, has very little to do with the generic approach to marketing in which we respond to advertised jobs, flood the market with direct mail, and go to the local chamber of commerce events. Creating wealth has everything to do with grouping and targeting clients by their predominant need, and designing your business to meet the need with vigor and strength.

WHO IS NOT MY CUSTOMER?

This is one of the toughest questions of all. When you believe on a deep level that bigger is better, as many of us do on a conscious or unconscious level, we find it very hard to say no to all but the real money-losers.

Do you conduct an annual analysis of projects by profitability? Most firms find that the things they are really expert in – amazingly – are the most profitable. Profile your clients by their Sparks Framework agendas and see if you can observe a pattern.

Now imagine a chain of components that your company offers. In industry, the traditional value chain begins with the company's core competencies, say making a beverage called Coke. Its value chain includes: 1) inputs and raw materials, 2) manufacturing its product, 3) distributing its product, and then 4) selling it to the customer.

In our industry, we begin with sales, then proceed to design, production, and construction phase services. Now layer on the less obvious links in the value chain: project management, code analysis and permitting, site analysis, public relations, team coordination, etc. Further layer on nontraditional services that we may offer

"Concentration on the smallest number of activities that will produce the highest amount of revenue is the key to economic results."

Peter F. Drucker

in-house or through an alliance: economic analysis, organizational design, strategic planning, real estate services, information systems design, market research, public process facilitation, etc.

As you dissect the client's psychology, you will learn that there are high, medium, and low value components in your mix. Perhaps there are several high-value components that are underdeveloped; perhaps some have negative value. For example, an Einstein doing detailed construction documents may not be valued by the client – in fact it may compromise his worth in the eyes of the client. A client who values the local access of a Community Leader may be skeptical of the same firm's supposed world-class technical expertise. A client seeking great program management may not value in-house design talent.

Think carefully about where you reap value in your value-chain, and with what classes of clients. Then create a list of colleagues and friends (perhaps competitors) that you can refer the mismatches to. Believe in abundance, since what goes around comes around.

THE SERVICE AND QUALITY TRAP

When you make your analysis about the willing client and his highest value agenda, beware of an unconscious assumption that runs rampant through the industry. According to our research, 85 percent of design firms believe that what makes them special, and what the client most values, is either service or quality, or both.

The phrase "meet and exceed client expectations" is contained in almost every mission statement we see. "Service," "excellence," and "high quality" are used literally everywhere. How do clients judge quality, in the absence of clear, statistical information? Answer: They can't. What they can do, however, is make the leap from a firm's distinctive expertise to the perception of high quality, based on deep know-how. "They must be good; that's what they're known for."

Firms generically citing quality and service are asking for a diluted position in the marketplace, a position that misses connecting with what the client truly values. Today both quality and service are *expected* of any design firm. They are no longer differentiators; they are prerequisites. After all, who doesn't want service? (When asked, wouldn't you like to have a few servants?) And who doesn't want good quality? We need to push beyond what are now hackneyed phrases.

In Chapter Two, Drivers of the Economy, we discussed the dynamics of the commodity market that emerged in the '80s. Our industry responded to the problem of high substitutability with what many practitioners believe to be bona fide professional – even moral – virtues: service and quality.

But these virtues, at their core, are pragmatic commercial strategies of enhancement – economic constructs. Looking at history, we can see that by 1910, John Wanamaker, "peer among merchants," and his fellow entrepreneurs had translated service into a powerful merchandizing tool that literally transformed the retail sector from the mundane to the (value-added) pleasurable. Certainly Japan's quality revolution in the past few decades provided considerable economic utility.

Through market evolution, quality and service have become basic societal values. They are the hallmark of civilized people, like good manners. Everyone is better with them than without them.

As a wealth-builder, your goal is to solve the client's most critical problems. *Don't let today's cliches confuse the issue for you.*

In his classic work on what motivates people, Frederick Herzberg formulated the theory of "hygiene factors and motivation factors." Motivation factors include achievement, recognition, and the work itself. Hygiene factors include money and working conditions. Hygiene factors do not positively motivate, but they can be detrimental if lacking. Today service and quality are essential hygiene factors; if they're missing, the client will be unhappy. Provide more than necessary, and it's probable that the added value won't be noticed.

There is one specific exception to the rule: *extraordinary service.*

Some clients under some conditions will pay a premium for a *much* higher level of service if they perceive a *much* higher value. For example, you might give long-term clients a preferred status among the firm's more sporadic clients.

In the design profession, Gerry Gerron's Seattle-based architectural firm, G2 Architecture, is an example of an extraordinary service strategy. "Treat your clients with exquisite care," he says, and they will become for you an annuity that keeps paying off. "It's just that simple," he continues. "Clients frequently call us in the evenings, weekends, Sunday mornings, whenever. If a client wants to talk, or he or she has an idea, we are always accessible. It's a true personal orientation on our part." Sounds a bit idealistic, perhaps, but the gritty underlying premise is that G2 is *extremely selective in its client base*. In fact, principal Gerron estimates that they accept only 40% of the commissions offered them.

Most of us, however, don't really intend to provide *extraordinary service*. We just mean returning phone calls in a timely way, meeting our agreements, and being attentive to clients as people. If you really want to be known for service, you must take it to a much higher level indeed.

ONE-STOP SHOPPING

Many clients think they want one-stop shopping, and many firms believe this is what every client wants. But give the one-stop premise a hard look, recalling that department stores have suffered financially in the wake of low-end Wal-Marts and high-end specialty shops, catalogs, and e-commerce. Consider also that government and corporate clients have largely cleaned house of their facilities (and other) departments, because they can get them cheaper and more effectively through outsourcing.

A bona fide full-service strategy can be effective for some firms, as long as you understand the underlying value that your client is paying for.

For example, if you are a Market Partner with a full-service strategy, establish it with the guiding caveat that your overall goal is the intimate, long-term client relationship, achieved through a range of services targeted to a certain market—not diversification. If you are an Orchestrator with a full-service strategy, recognize the supremacy of your project management expertise, which can be proven through your turnkey production track record. If you are a Community Leader with a full-service strategy, be sure to respect your overriding strategic position as the most committed firm in your community.

Sometimes what clients ask for and what they value most are two different things. Give yourself permission to be something other than a one-stop-shop if it makes sense for you. And seriously consider building a network of alliance partners that you can outsource yourself for the second-tier or complementary work.

INTERNATIONAL PRACTICE

The loud cheers you hear are the songs of focused firms, as markets go global. Walt Disney, for example, is wrestling with how best to procure design services internationally. Its conclusion, as others have learned, is to bring a proven, expert performer across the shores, and ally them with a local firm.

To operate on an international basis, firms must be executing a specialty at its best *and* know their target client's psychology. Whether managing huge, complex logistical problems, like the Kuwait fires that Bechtel handled, the special water supply problems of San Juan, Puerto Rico that Black & Veatch solved, the rollout of our nation's Wal-Marts that BSW produced, or the world's tallest office building in Singapore that Cesar Pelli put his signature on, the point conveys.

All the pros agree: master your specialty and select your client, because international practice adds increased demands from many other quarters.

CREATING WEALTH

Chapter Five

Creating Wealth
Principle Three:

Systematic Innovation

"The entrepreneur," said Jean-Baptiste Say, the French economist who coined the word around 1800, "shifts economic resources out of an area of lower productivity and into an area of higher productivity and greater yield." Today, most of us think of entrepreneurship and innovation as closely related. Some of us even think of innovation as something related to new computer technology.

But innovation in fact is much broader: *Innovation is the job of creating value by exploiting some form of change.*

Certainly it includes advances in equipment, process, and materials, but it can also include new techniques in staffing, marketing, policy, forecasting, ownership, and a host of other areas as well.

"What all the successful entrepreneurs I have met have in common is not a certain kind of personality but a commitment to the systematic practice of innovation."

Peter F. Drucker
*Innovation and
Entrepreneurship:
Practice and Principles*

Innovation is not about something *you* haven't done before, like starting a new business venture or transferring a new method from another firm to yours. Nor is innovation the same as invention.

Innovation is about fostering new ideas, implementing them, and then bringing them to market.

The grand-scale business innovators are virtually household names. Think for a minute about Sam Walton, John Nordstrom, Walt Disney, Bill Gates, Jack Welch, Paul Hawken, Leon Leonwood Bean, and the companies they built through innovation.

Now think of the countless things that you and your colleagues have done better by challenging yourselves, being open to new means of problem-solving, and by taking the time to read and talk – both inside and outside the industry. Then think of all the ideas you've had that never went anywhere. What happened?

The most common reason great ideas get lost is that we are too busy with "real work" to sponsor them. Too busy reacting to problems. Too busy stoking the machine. Adding to the time/real work dilemma, some of us have a thin financial cushion and a phobia about risk.

The Technology Gap

Clearly, the development of new ideas and technologies is linked with personal, company, and national wealth.

All great successes, including winning wars, mining valuable resources, enjoying a low unemployment rate, and advancing education are the direct result of breakthroughs in know-how: new technologies. Historically, economic theory held that land, labor, and capital were the factors of wealth. Yet countries like Brazil and Russia with vast natural resources have failed to become prosperous, while countries like Japan and Indonesia with few natural resources have created great wealth. The ability to develop (not necessarily invent) new technologies is the key.

The cache of unimplemented, but almost ready-to-go innovations is the new indicator of wealth. This technology now replaces land, labor, and capital. For our firms, this means that the *ability to produce new and better ways* of doing things, whether great or small, and when driven by the firm's focus, is the engine of wealth creation.

One of the quintessential examples of innovation is Intel. Andy Grove, Intel chairman and the 1997 *Time Magazine* Man of the Year, said, "We've built an organization that's like an athlete – tuned to play a particular sport." Intel's demanding culture of next-generation technologies has resulted in one of the most valuable firms in the world.

A study conducted by Manchester University in Britain likened the process of innovation to a "continuous track race," rather than the linear pipeline effect of R&D input and new product output. The study found that success in the market came not from just winning an innovation sprint, but from being a firm that produced a sustained "trajectory of improvements."

The Client: Inspiration for Innovation

Where do all your great ideas come from? If you're like most of us, they start with your clients' problems, ranging from real estate and funding issues to scheduling, production, and operational concerns. Sometimes they come from angry citizens or the political shenanigans in Washington. New ideas are always motivated by unsolved problems.

New York City-based HLW International took an unsolved problem by the horns when it accepted the challenge by Ciba-Geigy to be part of a design/build laboratory project in which all the profit for the designer was at risk. In addition to schedule and cost incentives and penalties, Ciba-Geigy's project manager George Batcher wanted to go a step further, to make a portion of the firm's profit at risk in the area of quality. "Every time I talked to a firm," he said, "they were on this quality bandwagon….You could hear the tune over and over… Sounds good, but it has no words." So Batcher created a user-satisfaction incentive.

This radical idea, and the subsequent acceptance by HLW, hit the *Wall Street Journal*, among others. The deal: in order to reach a $100,000 "enhanced profit" for quality, HLW had to undergo a rigorous survey and vote by end users after move-in. The requirement? A 75% satisfaction rate. HLW received an 84% vote, and took home its prize.

Bottom Duvivier, a high-tech interior design and architecture firm in Redwood City, California, develops proprietary facility programming technologies tuned to its high-tech client base including Intel, Sun

Microsystems, and Sega. In sync with the firm's "3T" software, for example, is an interactive instrument though which clients anywhere in the world can input their "task, time, and tool" needs for synthesis into scenarios and programs.

The building industry, like the aircraft, automobile, and telecommunications industries, produces products that are complex systems and thereby virtually impossible to reinvent completely. Instead, progress comes incrementally, stimulated by the wishes or complaints of valued clients. Progress also is stimulated by new offerings from suppliers, who fund most of the industry's R&D, to produce next-generation materials such as carbon fiber reinforcing and composites.

Although they stimulate innovation, clients rarely supply new ideas directly. Indeed the client may reject a new idea because it's not familiar. For example, in the 1980s, American companies missed the opportunity to lead the way in fax technology. Relying heavily on market research, they effectively asked, "Would you buy a telephone accessory that costs upwards of $1,500 that enables you to send, for $1 a page, the same letter the post office delivers for 25 cents?" American customers replied in the negative.

But the Japanese recognized that the customer is a lens by which to focus the opportunity. Customers wanted increased speed in communications, and Japanese companies proceeded to dominate the industry.

Wealth-creating firms do not make a virtue of stability and equilibrium, as do some highly trained professionals. Wealth creators value organizational health, of course, but they also understand what Austrian econo-mist Joseph Schumpeter called *creative destruction*. This force is a natural precursor to the innovation process. In its wake lies opportunity.

The Staff: Inspiration for Innovation

"The advance of technology is determined by our ability to exchange and process information."

Paul Zane Pilzer
Unlimited Wealth: Theory and Practice of Economic Alchemy

Perhaps the most powerful reason for focusing your ex-pertise is to enhance the firm's ability to *exchange and process information* so that people can learn from experi-ments and mistakes, incubate and develop interesting ideas, extract problem-solution knowledge from front line work with clients, and make better and faster decisions.

The "learning organization" is a very real technology for getting at innovation.

Learning organizations demand that time be invested for kicking around new ideas, both formally and infor-mally, in the hopes of generating advances. All that is needed is the sanction. For example, from the very beginning, 3M expected each employee to spend 10% of his or her time thinking about new ideas. Some of the most distinguished management consulting firms close on Friday afternoon so as to make time for pro-vocative speakers, sharing new ideas, and reporting on lessons learned during the week (they don't go home early!). This mentality is largely missing from our pro-fessions today.

Peter Senge's books, especially *The Fifth Discipline Fieldbook,* offer good tips and techniques for imple-menting a learning organization. But the main point to understand is this: make some time sacred, like an important project for an important client. Set aside an hour every Friday afternoon, or whatever time works best for your firm, for a frequent, regular gathering. Do not wait for the annual workshop where the juices may not be flowing on cue. With a sustained effort, a tremendous dialogue can take place that both generates innovation and supports individual and group progress.

Beyond internal resources, sparks can also come from cross-fertilization with outsiders who are focused on the same problems. Managing principals in our industry, for example, have created an association to develop their leadership skills, the Professional Services Management Association. The Advanced Management Institute brings together individuals seeking to expand their knowledge in various practice areas. And certainly the professional societies offer peer forums for exchanging ideas. Although some of us will naturally be good company leaders, those who participate at this concentrated level are more likely to exchange and process information about what works and what doesn't – faster – and then make innovative advances.

HOW THE SPARKS CULTURAL ARCHETYPES APPROACH INNOVATION

Each of the Sparks cultural archetypes naturally gravitates to market positions on the product life cycle curve. These firms know themselves, including their most valued expertise, and the agendas of their client base. They can easily identify where they most frequently operate on the curve.

"Ultimately, organizational learning is about creating something new."
Peter Senge
The Fifth Discipline

The good news is that each of the archetypes has plenty of room for innovation. Rather than losing themselves in the commodity market as they age, the cultural archetypes all participate in the "continuous track race" of new and better.

■ *The Einsteins will be inventing brand new services, markets, and styles.* They'll be experimenting in the design studio, the R&D team, and PhD group. Some rely on agencies, nonprofit foundations, and other sources of grants; others on wealthy clients to maintain their creative environment.

■ *The Niche Experts will be inventing new ways to apply the experimental work of the Einsteins.* They'll be looking for clever new ideas (and failed ideas) from many sources, building their expertise, and expanding their market base. They'll take the work being done in less regulated countries and other industries, translating for their niche.

■ *The Market Partners will be inventing new ways to cement the partnership relationships within their target market(s).* This includes new ways to get in front of target clients as a leader, as well as scouting out new services that might serve more client needs and integrating them into the mix. Some will seek acquisitions to add new bench depth.

■ *The Community Leaders will be inventing new ways to contribute to their community and personal relationships.* Look for Community Leaders to spearhead new city initiatives, new social causes, or new committees of their chosen civic, business, and cultural boards. Look for clever visibility as well, new real estate ventures, and perhaps a drive for new branch offices.

CULTURES	CLIENT AGENDA	INNOVATION
Einstein	Image, prestige	New services and techniques
Niche Expert	Special problem area	New applications of existing experiments to the niche
Market Partner	Trusted partner integration	New ways to cement the partnership
Community Leader	Access and service	New ways to contribute to the community and build relationships
Orchestrator	Control of complexity	New techniques to advance project management
Builder	Price and product	New technologies for cost-effectiveness

■ *The Orchestrators will be inventing new techniques to advance their project management skills.* This group will be gleaning ideas from Silicon Valley, reading *Fast Company*, and learning the latest from their business school grads. Some will be inventing the next generation of project/program/construction management.

■ *The Builders will be inventing new technologies to work their process more efficiently and cost-effectively.* Like other archetypes, they will be on top of computer technology. But Builders will find an added innovation path through

Life Cycle Phase	Phase I: Emergence	Phase II: Growth	Phase III: Early Stability	Phase IV: Late Stability	Phase V: Early Maturity	Phase VI: Late Maturity
Cultural Type	Einsteins	Niche Experts	Market Partners	Community Leaders	Orchestrators	Builders
Primary Driver	Invention of new theories and technologies	Advancement of niche through application of latest ideas	Immersion in selected industry or client type	Immersion in the locality: politically and socially	Project management: speed and logistics	Production of quality, cost-effective product

Copyright ©1999 Sparks: The Center for Strategic Planning

Each archetypal culture naturally gravitates to a certain position on the life cycle curve, reflecting the goals of the firm and its chosen client base. Innovation is required in each position.

their ISO 9000 quality programs which include structured processes for improvement. They'll also be leading the way in prefabricated construction, improving manufactured building materials, designs, and techniques.

Innovation and The Life Cycle Curve

To innovate, you need a firm grasp of your position on the life cycle curve. One of the biggest strategic mistakes made today is unknowingly following a market into a stage in the life cycle where the firm's culture no longer matches what's needed in the mature market. This is why so many traditional firms are unable to make design/build work for them profitably. Their culture just doesn't allow for the business orientation of the Orchestrator. It's why Nichers get so frustrated when the client hires a Community Leader. Their niche-oriented culture doesn't allow for the local hand-holding that is needed.

To remain focused on a market that at one time was successful for you, and now has changed, is nothing short of foolish.

Consider volume retail rollouts. If your firm is set up to reward original design, by definition it hasn't been bodybuilding its project management and production systems. It probably has more of a professional staff than a technical staff. Even if you want to follow your old-line clients into multi-location rural sites, you may not be able to deliver unless you redesign your company and its culture to fit their migrating definition of value.

"Men give me some credit for genius. All the genius I have lies in this: When I have a subject at hand I study it profoundly. Day and night it is before me. I explore it in all its bearings. My mind becomes pervaded with it. Then the effort which I have made is what people are pleased to call the fruit of genius."
Alexander Hamilton

Value always migrates from left to right on the product life cycle curve due to the constant evolutionary dynamics of products, services, and markets. The very momentum of the life cycle means that you have to choose where to play. Do you continue with your market as it ages or do you gradually replace that market with a new one that fits your firm's existing culture?

This is one of the most profound strategic questions in company design. The single, most fundamental question the firm must answer is the choice of one of three paths:

1) Follow the market as it matures and change the organization to fit the market's new requirements.
2) Sustain one of the cultural positions, and change markets as new ones emerge and old ones decline.
3) Free up new ventures from the traditional culture through spin-offs or spin-outs.

Whatever your decision, you can see how dependent the tremendous effort of innovation is on having a clear identity and a cadre of willing clients. The only real mistake is NOT choosing what to focus on.

For more on company design and decision-making, please refer to the other books in our series.

More Inspiration for New and Better

In *Innovation and Entrepreneurship*, Peter Drucker says that most innovations, especially the successful ones, result from a conscious, purposeful search for innovation opportunities. Diamonds can be found when certain situations are mined. Within the company or industry, try brainstorming unexpected occurrences, incongruities, process needs, and market changes. Outside the company, look for demographic changes, changes in perception, and new knowledge.

"The first law of modern business is no longer 'find a need and fill it,' but imagine a need and create it."
Paul Zane Pilzer

1. **Unexpected occurrences:** In the 1930s, IBM developed the first modern accounting machine, expecting it to be sold to banks. But banks had little money for new equipment at that time, so IBM found an unexpected market in New Deal-funded libraries. Fifteen years later, when everyone thought computers were for research, business unexpectedly showed an interest. Univac, which had the most advanced computers, spurned business applications, but IBM found its market.

   The unexpected failure is also ripe ground for innovation. Edsel is the classic example of the forerunner of the Mustang. Gene Kohn's first attempts were a learning ground for the acclaimed Kohn Pederson Fox.

2. **Incongruities:** Whenever an industry has an incongruity such as a growing market but falling profit margins, like the steel industry did, it's open for an innovation such as mini-mills. Cataract surgery was ripe for innovation when only one manual procedure (cutting a ligament) was left. Bill Conner of Alcon Labs added preservative to an enzyme that dissolved the ligament, and the rest was financial history.

The growth of design/build responds to an incongruity between the traditional separation of entities and the potential for greater efficiencies in a new format. HOK Sport was launched from an incongruity between existing employment situations and the vast potential in a new organizational format.

3. **Process needs:** The Media as we know it today began in the 1890s with the filling of two critical gaps in the process: Ottmar Mergenthaler's Linotype machine and modern advertising, invented by Joseph Pulitzer and William Randolph Hearst. In our industry, how many firms have found a need to move "up the deal-stream?" Many of us feel hemmed in by our position in the building process, and we seek more leverage and control by creating services that bring us closer to actually *becoming* the client. For example, CH2MHill developed a capital group, CAPCO, and Parsons created Parsons Development Company to move into a financial position on its projects.

Lunar Design, an industrial design firm in Palo Alto has moved off the "fee for services treadmill" and now structures part or all of its design fees to include equity in its clients' companies. At revenues of $8 million per year, Lunar employs 40 people. Yes, they deal with short-term risks and trade-offs, but their increased profitability through equity has yielded great results. Staff members are more passionate and energetic about their work, there is more room for experimentation, and they have time for some of that wished-for pro bono work.

Some firms like the Cambridge, MA–based Stubbins Associates have developed a bona fide project research expertise in-house in order to move upstream in the design process.

Other firms have created an "institute for the study of..." For example, Watkins Hamilton Ross in Houston, Texas formed the Center for Innovation in Health Facilities, a not-for-profit organization in 1997. The Center promotes research, conducts surveys, publishes books, and provides a national clearinghouse on best practices in the design, planning, and operation of healthcare facilities.

4. **Industry and market changes:** American health care has experienced a massive restructuring as HMOs and a host of independent surgical centers, psychiatric clinics, emergency centers, and cancer centers have opened throughout the country. Advances in telecommunications and distance learning are revolutionizing the higher education market. The fastest growing university, the University of Phoenix, doesn't have a campus at all.

The Internet allows for massive public input on projects, cheap construction documents prepared in India using shared proprietary web sites, a whole new approach to recruiting, and all kinds of electronic lawsuits. Remember when it was against the code of ethics to advertise? Now it's the rare firm that doesn't have a formal marketing program.

5. **Demographic changes:** Opportunities made possible by demographics are the least risky of all entrepreneurial pursuits. The recreational and sports market, for example, is one of the strongest markets of the future. As the Baby Boomers age – at 75 million, they are the largest and most affluent generation in history – they will require more and more recreational choices. Consider Club Med's success, resulting from the large numbers of affluent and educated young adults in Europe and the U.S. Note Wimberly Allison Tong & Goo's impressive international success in the resort hotel market. This will easily last for the next 20 or 30 years.

6. **Changes in perception:** Is the glass half full or half empty? Although Americans' health has improved in the last 20 years, the mood is more negative and avoidance-driven. Thus the explosion of health magazines, health foods, and exercise equipment. Although the computer was viewed as a threat not long ago, now everyone needs the newest and latest to do their taxes, talk to their friends, or just do work. Many of our regulatory-based markets result from political pressure born of citizen perception. And most all of our industry's environmental firms can thank citizen outcry for their very existence. Ask yourself, "What are people emotional about?"

Scott Carde, of Carde Ten Architects in Santa Monica, scans the papers for galvanizing public issues, such as homelessness, violence, and school test scores, for early indications of potential tax-supported building projects.

7. **New knowledge:** Those innovations based on new scientific, technical, or social knowledge are the superstars of entrepreneurship, but they are complex and risky to bring to market successfully. Ford was successful when they recognized a social change called "lifestyles" and designed the Mustang. DeHaviland was not successful when it invented the jet, but missed the users' needs (Boeing and Douglas picked up those pieces). In our industry, T. Y. Lin founded his firm to apply his research in prestressed concrete technology. This new knowledge launched an international practice and a revolution in bridge design.

When all is said and done, says Drucker, what innovation requires is hard, focused, purposeful work rather than genius. Innovation, he said, requires "knowledge, ingenuity, and focus in a well-defined area of endeavor."

Innovation isn't just for firms in Silicon Valley. Design firms of all types must systematically generate new and better ideas if they want to sustain a valuable position in the market. Principals and owners who aspire to wealth creation must nurture the learning impulse, and support their staff with real resources.

THINK AGAIN ABOUT SPIN-OFFS

New ideas are born of an effort to gain advantage. Students of evolution trace this dynamic to Charles Darwin's observation that new species are created when the right mutation meets the right environment. The woodpecker, for example, evolved mutations such as a long beak, balancing tail, and stronger claws that make it better than most birds at finding insects in tree bark.

What this means to us is that mutation, and subsequent division, may be a more effective market strategy than the popular strategies of acquisition, conglomerization, diversification, and convergence.

"What it's all about is management focus... that's what this split is about... What you've got now is everyone playing to their fore- hand."

Steve Sanger
Chair and CEO,
General Mills

Lots of examples abound, but the evolution of the computer is vivid. From the huge Univac evolved the mainframe, from the mainframe the PC, from the PC the laptop, notebook, and Palm Pilot. This evolutionary principle is at odds with the increase in mergers and acquisitions across all industries that we've seen over the past few years. Some work well, usually when they are very well aligned in values and goals. But they are rarely fertile ground for creating new value. In *Break Up: How Companies Use Spin-offs to Gain Focus and Grow Strong,* author David Sadtler and his Ashridge Strategy Group identify the problem: getting big and diverse causes value *destruction.* Among the problems:

- Lack of fit between owner and owned
- Executive vs. front line decision-making
- Friction among units rather than hoped-for synergy
- Corporate center bias
- Policies suited to one situation, required for all
- Loss of acquisition premiums, managing overvalued purchases
- Dilution of focus
- Sacrifice of innovation for short-term performance

Perhaps it's time to consider some new options beyond expansion. If spin-offs are anywhere on your radar screen, consider the following findings from international investment firm J.P. Morgan. In a study conducted on the stock market value of 77 spin-offs, the average spin-off performed 25 percent better than the stock market, and the smaller spin-offs beat the market by 45 percent.

Writing in *Inc. Magazine*, Bill Gross, a venture capitalist and business incubator, has outstanding results with "spin-outs" versus "spin-offs." His own experience as owner of an educational software firm called Knowledge Adventure, showed him the tremendous value of "letting go." When a team developed a breakthrough technology, his natural urge was to continue controlling what might be a hot property and its potential revenue stream – even though the firm's culture and systems weren't set up for this kind of venture. His board forced him to give majority ownership to the development team, and now he's a 19.9 percent owner of a $77 million business rather than an 80 percent owner of a $5 million business. This "counterintuitive arithmetic," says Gross, "causes the magnification of human potential. Giving employees near total equity unleashes a new level of performance, building economic value that more than makes up for any loss of control."

Although Gross, like most CEOs, initially wanted to grow the total entity, another phenomenon is taking shape: CEOs of big firms want to be creative again. Alex Mandl, formerly president and COO of AT&T, jumped ship for Telegent so he could stop spending all his energy on the "power struggles, budget debates, and political issues," and do something front line. Jim Barksdale, formerly CEO of AT&T, jumped ship for start-up Netscape. John Scully, CEO of Pepsi, jumped ship for start-up Live Picture. Christos Cotsakos, CEO of AC Nielson, jumped for start-up E*Trade.

"My half-baked reading of history is that we continue to go through these waves of entrepreneurial explosion followed by merger and consolidation. Out of that comes big, sluggish companies that eventually collapse under the weight of what they've created, and are killed off by the next wave of entrepreneurs."

Tom Peters

In the design professions, how many innovations have occurred in the large, highly diversified firms? Not many. In fact, most advances seem to occur when entrepreneurs are set free. Recall how construction management spun out of CRS, how waves of brilliant designers spun out of SOM, how legions of MBEs and WBEs spun out of old-boy firms, and how most operations and maintenance divisions spun out of environmental engineering practices. They divided off from the original organism that may still be functioning *very well*, and they grew to become strong, although different, offspring.

Askew Nixon Ferguson Architects in Memphis finds the spin-out strategy very effective, and in fact is working on their third such venture. Says Lee Askew, "If we made these new ideas into traditional company divisions, they would wither and die. Spun out, the development team gets charged up over 'their baby.' They have their own name, their own identity, and a high percent of equity. Ideally, we aim for a 25 percent (us) and 75 percent (them) split. They think big, and they grow into their vision quickly." ANFA's two spun-out entities, On-Line FM and CM Plus have reaped high rewards for the firm.

Another example is Archibus, a top-selling facilities management software spun-out from Jung/Brannen's R&D group. Set free to sink or swim, the firm built an enviable position as "best in class" of CAFM, and has over 50,000 users managing over 16 billion square feet of space.

In 1997, Harvey Stone spun off Stone Consulting and Design from a solid Community Leader firm in northwestern Pennsylvania. The new company is a niche practice focused on railroads, with micro-niches in tourist rail lines and downtown trolleys. Although the railroad expertise existed in embryo form within its previous organization, the separation paved the way for a clear identity, a cohesive culture, and a growing international practice.

Ideally, spin-outs result from far-sighted strategic planning. But in reality, many are catalyzed by dissatisfaction, such as a poor cultural fit, a failed acquisition, or just a healthy, strong-minded entrepreneur wanting a little freedom. These conditions, just like the problems that spark innovation, can create real value if managed well. And good strategic planning can harness these forces to the advantage of all parties.

Are you protesting emotionally? Yes, at first blush it looks like *getting smaller*, and this goes against the conventional grain. But to the extent that you keep your eye on your prime expertise, and let other enterprise ideas blossom on their own, you'll reap higher benefits for both the mother-ship and her spin-outs. Creative independence can indeed build wealth.

CREATING WEALTH

Chapter Six

Creating Wealth
Principle Four:
Credibility

When you have the first three elements of wealth creation in alignment – expertise, a willing client base, and a penchant for the new and better – the fourth principle, credibility, tends to follow naturally. But sometimes we neglect the last 25 percent of the equation.

"Diamonds are nothing more than chunks of coal that stuck to their jobs."
Malcolm Forbes

LIES, DAMNED LIES, AND STATISTICS

There's a common language that everyone understands. Not French, Spanish, or English. *It's statistics.* When you give facts about your performance and its results, the client responds with greater confidence. When you explain an occurrence or behavior, statistics validate your understanding. When you use rules of thumb to support a position, you build trust.

What makes clients really stand up and take notice is linking your performance, in empirical terms, to the client's own definition of success. When everyone else is dishing out hype, you offer "proof." Below are some powerful examples from design firms:

- Originally an interior design firm, spAce, consults to "high growth/high change corporations." The firm provides its clients up to 30 percent overall space savings and up to 90 percent reduction in cost to change (churn) space as a result of its expert replanning services.

- Leo Daly's energy-saving design for Lockheed Building 157 in Sunnyvale, California yielded a productivity increase of 15 percent and a reduced absenteeism rate of another 15 percent. Lockheed also claims to have won a $1.5 billion contract as a result of happier employees.

- Gianni Longo of American Communities Partnership spearheaded the Chattanooga, Tennessee Vision 2000 plan. Over a period of ten years, this program generated over $793 million in development projects in that community.

Early in my career I learned the secret of statistics. I was an associate at SOM in the early '80s, and we were working with a large oil company client. The client team gave us some background literature, featuring the company's latest achievement: "the most energy efficient building in the world." Being interested in this line of thinking, not to mention naïve, I said, "Gosh, how did you know it was the most energy efficient building in the world? How did you measure it? Did you send a team of researchers out to study the field?"

A big gun from corporate turned to me and replied, "Well, dear, we just *said it*." Stunned, I asked, "What if somebody challenges you, say one of your competitors?" The profound answer came: "No problem. Nobody can prove it's *not* true. At worst, we'll just back down."

I hope this is an extreme situation, but it's true that on occasion, people spin statistics.

Firms that are ranked number one in something enjoy a highly credible position. For example, according to *Engineering News-Record's 500*:

- Parsons Brinckerhoff is the nation's number one transportation firm.
- HOK is number one in sports.
- DMJM is number one in corrections.

Most of us, however, have to get more creative than this, generating the performance numbers ourselves. Set aside one-fifth of your marketing budget – it's that important – and spend it learning about your target client group's operating statistics and measures of success. Then you can craft your message accordingly.

An outstanding example of statistics as proof of exceptional design comes from Howard Wolff, corporate managing director of Wimberly Allison Tong & Goo. Resort designers based in Honolulu, the firm conducted a

"Providing architecture and engineering services is not valuable unless our clients' bottom lines (whatever that might be to the particular client) are enhanced."
George Theodore, CEO
Setter, Leach &
Lindstrom

study to measure how its 50 years of specialized hospitality design expertise translates into increased revenues for hotel owners and operators. The study covered seven years, used the industry's own yardsticks, and compared performance among comparable luxury hotels. WATG's work, they found, delivered its clients up to $61 higher average room rates, 4.1 percent higher occupancy rates, and $50 higher revenue per available room. (See www.watg.com, useful news:feature stories for details.)

Another level of statistical sophistication is the proprietary database. Think about all the surveys you've filled out over the years. Most get compiled into industry averages and sold back to you (at a discount if you filled in your form). Most run into the expensive $300 range, indicating that we value them.

Here are some specific ideas:
Because of our skills, our client...

... slowed personnel turnover to 4 percent,
... tripled land values,
... saved 40 percent of operating costs,
... sped planning board approval by 30 percent,
... gained 50 percent more publicity for the project,
... leased the building 5 percent faster,
... reduced nurse miles in the hospital by 45 percent,
... saved 25 percent of the project budget through skillful column design.

One way to build this database is to join with a client or two, or an association. Draper-Aden in Blacksburg, Virginia partnered with the Virginia Association of Counties and the Virginia Municipal League to research water and sewer rates for various municipalities in Virginia. They published their findings in a series of reports, and have continued the successful effort for several years now.

Lots of benefits accrue: getting closer to the client, creating industry benchmark statistics, and positioning your firm as the premier expert. Draper-Aden launched its environmental practice using this statistical information as leverage.

KPS Justice Group in Birmingham, Alabama, gleans statistics from their target client base via simple direct mail surveys. Statistics such as this: 70.1 percent (of justice officials surveyed) cite reduced costs of transporting inmates as the number one advantage of locating courts and jail facilities in a single justice center. This is a powerful way to say, "You should build one big justice center, and we're just the folks to help you."

In most cases, you already have a good sense of the results you need. You can capture the numbers if you just put in a small research effort. Ask your clients to conduct an internal study and provide manpower from your staff. Create a simple survey for them to fill out or respond to in an interview. If you have done a good job, your client will benefit too. Do not get hung up on perfectionism. An opinion poll is a legitimate statistical source. Even a ballpark estimate can be used to support your point.

"Wealth in America is more often the result of planning, perseverance, hard work, and most of all, self-discipline."

Thomas J. Stanley and
William D. Danko
*The Millionaire Next Door:
The Surprising Secrets of
America's Wealthy*

Another easy and fun way to get numbers is to conduct a focus group. I'm constantly amazed at how simple this is to do, and how interested people are in what might come out of it. Just ask away for your ratings, rankings, percentiles, and opinions.

Remember: Performance statistics are the expression of your value, based on what matters to your client. They must be collected, organized, defended (to your lawyers), and mainstreamed among staff.

Here are some example stats that the Sparks cultural archetypes might collect:

CULTURES	CLIENT AGENDA	STATISTICS
Einstein	Image, prestige	Drew 75 percent more visitors to the city
Niche Expert	Special problem area	Increased value of real estate holdings by 200 percent
Market Partner	Trusted partner integration	Won the client 16 industry awards
Community Leader	Access and service	Cut approvals time in half
Orchestrator	Control of complexity	Came in 50 percent faster than traditional
Builder	Price and product	Saved 30 percent on the construction cost

Once you realize the client's need for the common language, you'll seek opportunities for gathering statistics. Occasionally you might need to add a discrete disclaimer, but know that your clients are going to love having the ammunition *they* need when *their* committee wants justification.

THE BIG VOICE

A wealth-creating firm has a big voice. We do not mean a loud and brassy voice, but a dignified, refined presence on the client's radar screen. In Richard Weingardt's tenure as ACEC president, he convened a blue ribbon panel on engineering success requirements for the future. The result, *"Seeing Into the Future: The I Book,"* includes a plea to develop a "passion for public relations."

The big voice has several real advantages:

    1) it brings you to front-of-mind awareness,

    2) it positions you as a leader, and

    3) it distinguishes you from the crowd.

Further, if you are committed to public relations – as opposed to advertising – your firm will enjoy the halo effect of third-party credibility.

Ed Friedrichs, president of Gensler, says, "We're anxious to have our work published so it's visible to prospective clients..." This visibility works not only by enhancing the firm's image with prospective clients, but with the firm's long-term clients as well. Most clients are proud to

"Competitive advantage means providing high value-added services using a singular competitive strategy and targeted visible positioning."
Michael Porter

be associated with firms worthy of publication. Most welcome joint speaking engagements, too.

Although they don't broadcast it, highly visible firms have either in-house PR or retain a PR consultant. Sverdrup has an infrastructure of "PR stars" throughout their organization. Centerbrook Architects, winner of the *1998 AIA Firm of the Year*, employs two full-time people working on publicity, within a staff of sixty-six. Duany Plater-Zyberk has a list of visibility evidence a mile long. According to their web page, the firm has been:

- Mentioned in 945 articles and 97 books
- Invited to present 366 lectures
- Given 52 awards, and
- Included in 40 exhibits

DPZ is a household name in urban planning circles, and clearly the most credible firm in its area of expertise.

CH2MHill was an early investor in "corporate communications." They blazed the trail with marketing legend Diane Creel at the helm along with her sizable staff in Seattle and Denver. Among their award-winning initiatives, CH2M produces one of the most substantive illustrations of technical expertise ever: *The Information Exchange.* Like an expanded reader-response card, this compendium lists articles, white papers, and lectures – by topic – from which the reader can request copies. Diane Creel has since become President and CEO of the global engineering technology firm, EarthTech. And she's recreated at EarthTech the impressive corporate communications juggernaut which works so well at CH2M.

Public relations is powerful, but like good medicine, you have to use it for it to work. Those who engage public relations consultants know that they require interesting and new information in order to get you publicized. They also require a clear, coherent description of who you are as a firm. This is a serious obstacle for those who cannot or will not decide on a focus.

If you're up on your expertise, no doubt you'll be doing something interesting, such as designing another high-profile project for Stanford, researching attitudes on toll road user fees, or leading a charge for better school facilities in the county. The press is interested in:

- Research and trends, along with statistics
- Innovations in a traditional process
- New public construction that will affect a lot of people
- A project for a highly visible client
- Controversial positions on any topic

The press is very interested in a strong viewpoint. Malcolm Pirnie, for example, has been fighting the privatization trend in water and wastewater treatment. The firm launched a highly visible campaign, "Storm Clouds on the Horizon" and "Our Declaration of Independence" to position itself as an independent design firm that represents its municipal clients' best interests. Its program highlights a potential conflict of interest posed by the big contractors, operators, and suppliers with whom many of its competitors have allied themselves.

Sample visibility strategies of the Sparks cultural archetypes are:

CULTURES	CLIENT AGENDA	VISIBILITY
Einstein	Image, prestige	Teaching at an Ivy League school
Niche Expert	Special problem area	Speaking at client conferences
Market Partner	Trusted partner integration	Writing industry trend newsletters
Community Leader	Access and service	Community fund-raising, boards and committees, local radio talk shows
Orchestrator	Control of complexity	Coverage in the business press
Builder	Price and product	Pointed direct mail and trade advertising

BRANDING

Branding is the newest technique in design firm marketing, yet it is basic in the product world. Branding is about naming something with the intent to "own" it in the marketplace. Xerox, Kleenex, and Coke are prime examples. Branding gives the buyer a shortcut in decision-making, because the brand is a known quantity and can be expected to perform well as a result. It gives the company a competitive edge because clients know that trading with a brand name rather than a generic reduces their risk of mistakes.

And of course, the more focused it is, the more potent it is. Certainly Honda, Toyota, and Nissan made powerful moves when they created the brands, Acura, Lexus, and Infiniti.

In our strategy courses we play a game called "Design a Great Firm." As part of the exercise, the new company has to have a ….name! *Never* have we said it can't be the principals' names, yet never has a group voluntarily selected personal names. Perhaps the selection of a descriptive name is a subtle design mechanism to keep the message clear?

- *"Atlantatude" is a design atelier with a unique southern style influence.*

- *"Global Eagle" is a golf clubhouse and resort community design firm, operating internationally.*

- *"Zeitgeist"* is a high-tech project management/construction management firm.

- *"ZipZap"* dominates the world of speedy retail rollouts.

- *"Design for Healthcare"* provides lifecycle services for hospital clients in the Midwest.

- *"Life Critical"* is a cutting-edge designer of emergency rooms and trauma centers.

- *"U.P. Community Design"* is part of every major project in the Upper Peninsula of Michigan, and is built on community participation.

- *"AirMax"* does design/build airport projects throughout the country.

Einsteins excepted, using the founders' names leaves room for un-strategic shenanigans: perceptual confusion and survivalist reactivity that can kill success. Clients have a huge range of choices, and few have time to wade through all the professional marketing communications. They want their decisions made easy, and the results made explicit and predictable.

In our profession, most firms entertaining this technique are hoping that their existing company name will do the trick and they can avoid a big statement about anything specific. Some dip their toe in, keeping the standard name and perhaps adding another to indicate a certain market or service. However, there's lots more potential. We see at least three levels of branding operating now in our industry.

In "Wide Band" branding, the company name is the brand, and it stands for something that has become known as the standard. For example, Parsons Brinckerhoff stands for transportation, and Bechtel stands for complex design/construct.

In "Medium Band" format, the brand is a specialty of the larger company, such as HOK Sport or Baker Environmental.

In "Narrow Band" branding, the company has a proprietary process or specialty, such as DPZ's "New Urbanism"; CRS/William Pena's programming technique, "Problem Seeking"; CH2MHill's wastewater treatment tool, the "Step-Feed Process"; or Brennan Beer Gorman's "Flash-Track System."

A company's name can reflect and support internal transformation as well, especially when the firm would like to boldly reposition itself with new and better clients. An excellent example is once-conservative Portland, Oregon architects, JKS, who metamorphosed themselves under CEO Gary Reddick's leadership in 1995. Now branded as Sienna Architecture, the firm lives up to its artistic, Italian city image. It has become a high-energy, high-visibility firm doing leading-edge design for such clients as Nike and Starbucks.

Go beyond the conventional. Take a stand and make some waves.

"Life is too short to be little."
Benjamin Disraeli

Writing the Book

Writing for client groups is a powerful credibility tool. Although a major commitment, writing a book is the ultimate tool for both launching and sustaining a top marketplace leadership position. Advice: conduct some original research, brand a new process, tell stories, and use lots of graphics. This sets the stage for the book to be reviewed in the client press (and purchased).

One of the best examples is Sarah Susanka's *The Not So Big House: A Blueprint for the Way We Really Live.* The firm targeted "people of average means," a group thought by many as difficult and untenable to serve, and turned them into a profitable and highly desirable clientele. Principal of Mulfinger, Susanka, Mahady & Partners in Minneapolis, Susanka has been named *Life Magazine's* Architect of the Year.

If the few publishers in our industry aren't your cup of tea, you can very respectably self-publish. In fact, many people now prefer self-publishing for the increased control of content and graphics as well as for better financial return. Lots of good options exist for co-publishing too, in which you create and market the book while the publisher manages inventory and fulfillment. School experts Fanning/Howey, for example, have completed three books in an ongoing series: *Community Use of Schools: A Facilities Design Perspective, Making a World of Difference: Elementary Schools,* and *Shaping the Future: Middle Schools.* (The fourth book will be about high schools.) Fanning/Howey has had rave reviews from the press, including cover stories in *School Planning and Management.* The firm has also enjoyed a strong response from its target clients, school superintendents. Company principals particularly love to use the books in interviews during question and answer time. Nothing like sending the message, "We wrote the book!"

TEN PRINCIPLES

Another credibility tool is a "Ten Principles List" (or however many you like). Only the masters are in a position to cut through all the hype and tell the client what really matters. When all is said and done, what factors are essential to achieving rave results in your area of expertise, for your clients?

Think of the eight principles of excellence espoused by Peters and Waterman in *In Search of Excellence.* You'll recall Steven Covey's world renowned list of seven habits and Deming's 14 points. How about Alcoholics Anonymous' twelve-step program? The Ten Commandments?

Generating a set of timeless principles indicates the depth of your commitment to your expertise, and sets you apart from everyone droning on about service and quality. Include your list in all your materials, and add to them as you read articles and observe more. Start small and build up the list over time. Consider the value of the list in staff training too.

By way of example, here's our list. We use it all the time, and continue to craft it as we go along.

GREAT STRATEGY
The SPARKS Principles

1. MOTIVATION
Forward change is leveraged by a definable problem, threat, or ambition. Virtually nothing gets done in the world because "we should." Action takes place because of discomfort. Welcome it.

2. FOCUS
What makes firms attractive is a strong, clear identity.
Power comes from point of view, conviction, and mastery in a focused area of endeavor. It is what makes great leaders and great organizations so memorable.

3. BOLDNESS
Great organizations have bold vision and purpose.
The number one characteristic of winning teams is their sense of destiny. This energizes and unifies effort, and brings groups beyond the realm of politics to real performance.

4. SCARCITY
Higher fees go to those with scarce expertise.
The law of supply and demand dictates that price improves with distinctive expertise, including project-type, service-type, and process-type specialties.

5. PARTICIPATION
Collaboration and participation yield higher commitment.
Only when people have been involved in some way can they commit energy and resources to a cause.

GREAT STRATEGY
The SPARKS Principles

6. MENTAL MODEL
A cohesive operating model promotes the strengthening of expertise.
Many firms sprinkle mixed messages over staff – it's not uncommon to tell
the same person *think out of the box* and *increase your utilization*. Both are
good, but hard to do equally well. Strategies must hang together.

7. GROOVES
Simple mechanisms and structures "naturally" program implementation. What undermines implementation is a long sequential list of tasks to
be completed. By translating strategy into new roles and processes, we
make doing the right things easy.

8. CHAMPIONS
Leaders who champion the firm's strategic plan get more results.
Steam in the engine doesn't happen by itself; it must be stoked. Strategy is
the core job of the firm's top leadership, from development and refinement
through committed cultivation.

9. GROWTH
Growth is essential.
Most often we think of growth in terms of size. Yet vigorous growth can also
occur in such areas as higher quality staff, more important projects, wider
geographical coverage, and increased profit.

10. THINK TIME
Great strategy requires thought.
Few great thoughts have been born while sitting at a desk, deadline at hand.
Strategic perspective requires setting aside time for inspiration, dialogue, what-
ifs, and debate.

A Lesson in Chemistry

*"I don't know,
we just had the right
chemistry with them."*
IBM

Confidence. Comfort Level. Trustworthiness. Chemistry. Have you heard these words said about *the other guys* when you came in second?

Experts are confident, comfortable, and trustworthy. They can take a little more risk to be personal and even humorous because they needn't concentrate so hard on their subject matter. That part is largely mastered. They reach out, almost effortlessly, to establish "chemistry," the feel-good magic of relationships.

We all know the old adage that "clients buy on emotion, and justify it later." In fact, our most ancient genetic programming gives us the ability to smell a friend – or a rat. We call it our *judgment* or our *intuition*, and it's a tool we all use to discriminate good from bad. We also call it trust.

Today, as in the past, selling anything as individualistic and complex as design services requires a commitment to forging strong client relationships. This *bridge across the intangible* applies to each and every one of the Sparks cultural archetypes. It's nothing short of basic hygiene in wealth creation.

Gensler is one of the most vocal proponents of building the high-communication/high-trust relationship as opposed to *serving* the client. Ed Friedrichs, Gensler president, says that the firm carefully builds and strengthens these relationships, but cautions that they need to be *with the right set of people*. He goes on to say that, "In terms of conventional marketing – people out on the street finding leads, knocking on doors, making acquaintances – we have *no one* doing that. Our marketing is through existing and repeat clients, along with referral business." When that happens both the consultant and the client are set to enjoy each other on projects that, in our industry, now average two years in length. No wonder relationship skills are so essential.

Seattle architect Gerry Gerron recalled his wedding several years ago. "We had 400 people. At one point, I looked out over the crowd gathered on our lawn, and was shocked to discover that some 80 percent of these friends began as clients."

This mix of the personal and professional is the single best way you can judge a valuable enterprise (as well as a life's career). Remember, however, that if you are good, you can achieve these results in any of the Sparks business designs. This point brings us back to Principle One: you've got to be good at something. No one will value you enough to sustain a personal relationship beyond a single project if you're not knowledgeable about – and committed to – the client's world.

Americans believe that for every problem there is a solution. Europeans believe that for every solution there is a problem. Inherent in the close client relationship is a potential pitfall: losing focus.

Have you ever experienced a situation in which the client gains such confidence in the firm that they send you all kinds of work? It's a mix. Some projects are right, but others are too small, or out of your expertise – but you are enjoying the relationship. You busy your staff producing the stew. Then, when the really great project comes in you have no one available. Inevitably, you shunt off the unwanted or too-difficult project to a junior staffer, with unsatisfactory results. This scene is common with poorly-matched referral projects as well.

Sometimes the work flows from a plum project to the follow-on housekeeping projects. If you don't keep your focus in mind, the client may begin to think of your firm as expert in service work, but not the guru for the next big event. Advice: keep your client relationship strong, but *keep clear about your priorities*. And review the section on spin-offs.

Since client chemistry is an essential tool of value-creation, and since most technical professionals are not schooled in the technologies involved, we recommend *Emotional Intelligence* by Daniel Goleman. Emotional intelligence (as opposed to IQ) is the capacity for recognizing and managing our own feelings and those of others, so as to reach our goals.

What some of us pass off as charm, chemistry, or great communication skills consists of five specific dimensions and 25 specific competencies that can be learned. The five dimensions are:

1. self-awareness
2. self-regulation
3. motivation
4. empathy
5. social skills

According to Goleman, "Technical skill is an entry-level requirement. You must have enough to do the job, but it's not what sets star performers apart." In a

Wired Magazine interview, Goleman cites a University of California at Berkeley study started in the 1950s that followed a group of PhD students in science and technical fields for 40 years. Findings showed that emotional intelligence abilities were four times more important than IQ in determining professional success and prestige.

The most common setting for client relationship-building is the meeting. A recent study published in *Successful Meetings Magazine* identified what qualities make executives most successful today. Consistent with the communication skills mentioned above, two specific characteristics emerged: 1) a sense of humor, and 2) the ability to run a great meeting.

Why? Because it's impossible to bring people together effectively while you're worrying about your own problems and ambitions. The output of meetings – ideas, decisions, and consensus – can be improved using very specific personal skills.

These skills *can* be learned. Imagine how much coaching Ronald Reagan, the great communicator, received. Get training, lots of training.

- Provide a Myers-Briggs Type Indicator workshop. The tool has been recently redesigned, and it works wonders in both understanding and managing all types of relationships.

- Stage an ongoing lunch program entitled, "Lessons I've Learned Dealing with Clients," to improve everyone's storytelling skills.

"Everything is about relationships – even the stock market reflects how people feel about each other."
Peter Drucker

■ Start a Toastmasters Program to desensitize your introverts by exposing them to practice situations.

The more your people understand themselves and others, the more you leverage all your wealth-creating investments.

Communication is perhaps the most difficult skill in the world. We avoid it because it's difficult, and in our technocratic and entrepreneurial value systems, we often pass it off as so much fluff.

But bad communication starts wars, ends partnerships, and causes lawsuits, not to mention loses you money. Strong communication skills yield repeat and referral work, and reduce marketing costs. The client cuts you slack when the inevitable problems arise. And good staff stays put.

TECHNOLOGY ASSISTS

While technology continues to make us more productive, it can also bring us closer together. Secure web sites for all project members let you share files, presentation graphics, and funny stories. Video-conferencing and video workshops as well as chat rooms for public process input are today's reality. The next generation of tools is focused on collaborative technologies, as biggies such as the Xerox Palo Alto Research Center (the people who invented the Macintosh) and MIT study technology-assisted innovation. In the near future, *interpersonal* computing will be much more pervasive than personal computing.

Teams and Alliances

Partnering, a technology for accelerating communications among team members, has enjoyed popularity among owners, most notably by the U.S. Army Corps of Engineers. In fact, the Corps credits partnering with tangible savings in time and money, not to mention decreased litigation. In the past five years, indefinite delivery contracts have taken hold with most federal and municipal agencies as well as institutions and companies such as Kaiser Permanente and Proctor & Gamble. These longer-term partnered teams rely on increased communication efficiencies to deliver their benefits.

Of course, what we call partnering has been an informal process used for many years. Today's hectic pace, however, has necessitated a more reliable, controllable methodology to get the job done quickly. In the *Third Wave*, Alvin Toffler predicted the 21st century as an "ever-changing mosaic" of firms linking and de-linking in the marketplace in order to deliver highly tuned expertise.

Teaming, which is driven by client demand for a more exact matching of project requirements and available expertise, will last well into the future. Firms such as Ellerbe Becket have for years had formal teaming agreements with Community Leader firms in many U.S. cities for health care projects, for example. Magellan Consulting has a brokering service that matches independent technical specialists with larger firms. This enhances project teams on an as-needed basis while providing corporate support for individual practitioners. And the Global Design Alliance with fifteen A&E members around the country, seems to be hitting its stride. Never before have we needed stronger communication skills.

THE PERSONAL EXPERIENCE

Beyond these networked alliances, an even more radical future prospect is the "experience economy." After commodities, goods, and services, memorable experiences are the next stage in the progression of economic value. Consider some clever examples from the business world as they pursue lasting customer relationships: Virgin and British Airways give their road warrior customers a soothing all-frills experience, Silicon Graphics' Visionarium brings customers and engineers together for a stimulating mental experience, and Borders marries the book and cappuccino experience.

Take everything you know about communications, relationship-building, and chemistry – and ratchet it up. Design an engaging personal experience for the client – or as Disney calls them, the guests.

Most of us are still fixated on the golf game, while the leading edge players like Pritzker Prize winner Renzo Piano stage exuberant workshops over the Internet to save ancient Italian churches. Mixed-use development consultants, Street-Works, designed a Monopoly game charrette for revitalizing downtown Charlotte, NC. RTKL's ID8 entertainment group uses storyboarding to structure the experience. Their highly successful Bayside Marina in Yokohama, for example, is woven around a fictional boy washed ashore from a shipwrecked Nantucket fishing boat.

Try this provocative question from the experience economy, "If you charged admission, what would it be for?" The serious wealth-builders will turn this fresh idea into a company retreat agenda item.

Finally, one of the real hallmarks of credibility is this: honesty. It's counterintuitive, perhaps, especially in the client service/servant game, but it establishes you as someone whose word can be relied upon.

I love a story like this one from Sheryl Maibach, VP of Barton Malow, one of the top general contractors in the U.S. She once asked a school client, "Why is it that you keep giving us so much work?" The client had one thing to say. "We think the world of your project manager, Charlie. He's the only guy we work with that has the guts to tell us *no* when something isn't in our best interest."

Credibility isn't about hype. Like Charlie, it's about knowing your stuff and feeling comfortable enough to take some risks and extend yourself personally. That's how long-term relationships are built. And long-term relationships are a capital asset in the wealth-creating firm.

A COROLLARY: COURAGE

My daughter Elliott had her first season of softball this year. Not being a great athlete myself, I was determined to expose her to "a better life" than my suburban girl upbringing in the '50s. So when I saw the ads, I took her kicking and screaming to the sign-up for Little League. "Little League is for boys," she insisted. "I can't do this." But she signed up, and she showed up.

After her first practice, Elliott came running up to me, breathless with excitement, sweaty, hair sticking out everywhere. "Mommy, mommy, I got picked to be a pitcher. Coach says I have an arm!"

Naturally, I started thinking about her future.... Orioles games, a pitching coach, playing catch after school, road tours. But on the way home, my little darling tells me how she wants to rent a movie, go online, call her friends, play some basketball, and have a party (with boys).

Has everyone given this lecture to their kids? "If you want to get good at something, you're going to have to … PRACTICE!" That's the secret of building skills, whether it's pitching, math, or a musical instrument. OR in the case of our firms, whether it's a certain project type, wired-in relationships in town, incredible project management, speed, or any kind of expertise. It's a fact of life that you're accorded more value when you can deliver more value – by doing something outstandingly well.

So the first game against the "Phillies" comes along. Elliott walks up to the pitcher's mound and starts throwing wild pitches. One is high, one is low, one is outside, one hits the kid in the leg. It got worse, and the coach somehow kept her in for the whole torturous game. It's rough on parents to see their frustrated and humiliated baby crying on the mound. The second and third games weren't much better. But things started to click in the fourth game. (And, of course, she's been *practicing* this whole time.) She gets up there. She leans forward and glares at the batter, then zips into her windup. BAM. BAM. BAM. She's striking them out. That's my daughter!!

Yes, it can be tough in the beginning, but she created value – for herself and for her team.

Our design firms are a lot like kids. So many opportunities, so many ways to grow, so many things we can be. Not enough time to master everything we want to do. We get spread so thin that we wind up an inch deep and a mile wide. In sports terms, we're weekend athletes, and we all know what that income is like, compared to, say, Michael Jordan.

In the design professions, HOK Sport demolished forever the idea of the great generalist firm. Not just a division of the big firm, HOK Sport was built with a separate mission, a separate name, a separate location, new people, and a separate structure. They became true leaders, using the principles of Focus, Client Selection, Innovation, and Credibility. How many design firms can you count that have enjoyed such leadership?

"Dream, believe, dare, do."
Walt Disney

Go make your dreams come true.

CREATING WEALTH

Top Ten Learning Questions
for Each Wealth Principle

What's the best way to work with the ideas offered in this book?

Most firms today have a learning program in place or are developing one. Most also have a strategic process that needs improvement. A deep dialogue about the wealth principles enriches both of these processes, bringing new life to retreat and management discussions.

Try this: Schedule a four-session *Creating Wealth* program using the learning questions as catalysts. The answers will stretch your strategic thinking muscles, and keep you future-oriented. They will clarify and strengthen your culture. They will form the basis of your strategic plan as well as your operating guidelines in marketing, project delivery, human resources, finance, and leadership.

Select a central discussion leader, or offer several individuals the opportunity to lead sections. Be purposeful in your debate. Actively manage it from brainstorming all the way through to consensus-building and decision-making. Appoint a scribe who will summarize the team's thinking for use in strategic planning as well as follow-on communication with the firm's stakeholders.

Using the learning questions, your mind *will* travel beyond the bounds of the firm's current mental operating model. Espouse a firmwide attitude of experimentation, and move ahead with courage.

SESSION ONE: Clarity of Focus

1. Which philosophies of good design appeal most to you?

2. Which niches are most attractive to you?

3. In which broad markets do you see the greatest opportunity?

4. What community might your firm dedicate itself to?

5. What about project management draws your satisfaction?

SESSION ONE (continued)

6. What opportunities in streamlined replication have pull for you?

7. What are the features and benefits of the above types of focus for your own firm?

8. Which firms are the leaders in each type of focus you mentioned?

9. Are there mixed messages you give your staff about what's really important to achieve (driving forces)?

10. What are the "marginal temptations" you currently have under consideration?

SESSION TWO: The Willing Client Base

1. Which clients have been your favorites in past years? Why?

2. Which types of clients get real value from your work?

3. What are their most critical problem agendas?

4. For what services will they pay the highest fees?

5. Which services can they acquire easily in the marketplace?

SESSION TWO: (continued)

6. Can these be supplied instead through alliance relationships?

7. Categorize your clients by their Sparks Framework agendas.

8. Profile the perfect client for your firm, including who is not right.

9. How do you feel about the "service and quality trap?"

10. What is your position on "one-stop-shopping?"

SESSION THREE: Systematic Innovation

1. Name three great ideas you've had in the past that were implemented.

2. Name three great ideas you've had that failed to be implemented.

3. What prevented you from their realization?

4. Name five things your (ideal) clients are frustrated about.

5. Can you find a way to make their lives easier?

136

SESSION THREE: (continued)

6. What organizations are focused on the same issues?
   (Should you start one?)

7. What would your Sparks Framework cultural archetype be
   inventing?

8. What changes can you observe in the marketplace?

9. If you were going to spin off/out a piece of your firm,
   what would it be?

10. What would a winning strategy look like for both the spin-
    out and "mother ship?"

SESSION FOUR: Credibility

1. What criteria do your ideal clients use to identify a successful project?

2. What statistics have you developed (or will you develop) to communicate your past success with these criteria?

3. How do you feel about taking a stand in the press on issues of concern to the firm?

4. What is your firm's hard-hitting, distinctive message that characterizes its communications?

5. What stories can you identify that are newsworthy?

SESSION FOUR: (Continued)

6. What condition is your "brand" in?

7. What should your book be about?

8. How much support do you provide for communication and relationship-building skills?

9. How well-organized is your network of team-members?

10. If you charged admission, what would it be for?

CREATING WEALTH

GREAT BOOKS

If you'd like to add more to your body of knowledge on wealth creation, the following books and articles are outstanding.

Business Strategy
- *The Experience Economy*, by B. Joseph Pine and James H. Gilmore, Harvard Business School Press, 1999.
- "How to Get Rich in America," by Edward O. Welles, *Inc.*, April 1999.
- *The Millionaire Next Door: Surprising Secrets of America's Wealthy*, by Thomas J. Stanley and William D. Danko, Longstreet Press, 1996.
- *The Profit Zone: How Strategic Business Design Will Lead You to Tomorrow's Profits*, by Adrian Slywotsky and David Morrison, Random House, 1997.
- *Top Management Strategy: What It Is and How to Make It Work*, by Benjamin Tregoe and John W. Zimmerman, Touchstone/Simon & Schuster, 1980.

Market Focus
- *Focus: the Future of Your Company Depends on It*, by Al Ries, HarperBusiness, 1996.
- *Positioning: the Battle for Your Mind*, by Al Ries and Jack Trout, Warner Books, 1981.

Innovation
- *The Dance of Change: the Challenges to Sustaining Momentum in Learning Organizations,* by Peter Senge, Currency Doubleday, 1999.
- *Innovation and Entrepreneurship: Principles and Practices*, by Peter F. Drucker, HarperBusiness, 1993.
- *The Fifth Discipline*, by Peter Senge, Currency Doubleday, 1990
- *The Fifth Discipline Fieldbook*, by Peter Senge, Currency Doubleday, 1994
- *Unlimited Wealth: the Theory and Practice of Economic Alchemy,* by Paul Zane Pilzer, Crown Publishing, 1991.

GREAT BOOKS

Spinning Off Businesses
- *Break-Up: How Companies Use Spin-offs to Gain Focus and Grow Strong,* by David Sadtler, et al, The Free Press, 1997.
- "The New Math of Ownership," by Bill Gross, *Inc.*, November-December 1998.

Building Communication Skills
- "Interview with Daniel Goleman," by Jeff Greenwald, *Wired Magazine*, December 1998.
- *Working with Emotional Intelligence*, by Daniel Goleman, Bantam Books, 1998.

Economics and Wealth Creation
- *Building Wealth: The New Rules for Individuals, Companies and Nations*, by Lester C. Thurow, HarperCollins, 1999.
- *The Wealth and Poverty of Nations: Why Some Are So Rich and Some Are So Poor,* by David S. Landes, W.W. Norton & Company, 1999.

Extraordinary Service
- *Raving Fans: a Revolutionary Approach to Customer Service*, by Ken Blanchard et al, William Morrow and Company, 1993.

INDEX OF DESIGN FIRMS AND INDIVIDUALS

GENERAL INDEX

CREATING WEALTH

Order copies of this book, as well as other books by Ellen Flynn-Heapes,
for your company retreats:

THE SPARKS FRAMEWORK:
A HANDBOOK OF VALUE CREATION STRATEGIES

THE SPARKS FRAMEWORK ASSESSMENT:
CHARTING YOUR PREFERENCES

MAKING IT REAL!
A STRATEGIC PLANNING PLAYBOOK FOR A/E/C
BUSINESS DESIGN AND TRANSITION

For easy ordering:

use the QUICK ORDER FORMS on the following pages

Quick Order Form

By Fax   (703) 838-8082

By Mail   SPARKS, P.O. BOX 205, ALEXANDRIA, VA 22313

Title	Price	Qty	Totals
Creating Wealth Principles and Practices for Design Firms	$29.95		
The Sparks Framework Assessment Charting Your Preferences (workbook)	$19.95		
Making It Real!* A Strategic Planning Playbook for A/E/C Business Design and Transition			
The Sparks Framework* A Handbook of Value-Creating Strategies			

10% discount on orders of 10 or more of each title

*Applicable sales tax, shipping, and overnight
delivery charges will be added. Payable in US dollars.*   **OrderTotal**

Overnight Delivery?   Yes   ☐   No ☐

Name _____   Job Title _____

Organization _____

Address _____

City/State _____   Zip Code _____

Phone _____   Fax _____   E-mail _____

☐ Visa   ☐ MasterCard

Name on Credit Card _____

Card Number _____   Expiration Date _____

Signature_____   Date _____

☐   **Please invoice us**   PO# _____

See us at www.ForSparks.com   *call for pre-publication pricing at (703) 838-8080

Quick Order Form

Title	Price	Qty	Totals
Creating Wealth Principles and Practices for Design Firms	$29.95		
The Sparks Framework Assessment Charting Your Preferences (workbook)	$19.95		
Making It Real!* A Strategic Planning Playbook for A/E/C Business Design and Transition			
The Sparks Framework* A Handbook of Value-Creating Strategies			

10% discount on orders of 10 or more of each title

Applicable sales tax, shipping, and overnight
delivery charges will be added. Payable in US dollars.   **OrderTotal**

Overnight Delivery? Yes ☐ No ☐

Name _____ Job Title _____

Organization _____

Address _____

City/State _____ Zip Code _____

Phone _____ Fax _____ E-mail _____

☐ Visa   ☐ MasterCard

Name on Credit Card _____

Card Number _____ Expiration Date _____

Signature _____ Date _____

☐ **Please invoice us**   PO# _____